PRAYERS
that Changed
HISTORY

PRAYERS
that Changed
HISTORY

R. EARL ALLEN

Broadman Press / Nashville, Tennessee

4282–52 (BRP)
4252–57 (Trade)
ISBN: 0–8054–5257–5 (Trade)

Scripture quotations marked (NASB) are from the *New American Standard Bible*, © The Lockman Foundation 1960, 1962, 1963, 1968, 1971, 1972, 1973, 1975, and are used by permission. Those marked (TLB) are from *The Living Bible, Paraphrased.* © Tyndale House Publishers, 1971. Used by permission. Those marked (RSV) are from the Revised Standard Version. © Division of Christian Education of the National Council of Churches of Christ in the United States of America, 1946, 1942.

Dewey Decimal Classification: 220.8
Subject headings: PRAYERS // PRAYER
Library of Congress Catalog Card Number: 77–71728

Printed in the United States of America

Dedicated
to my
favorite missionaries
Veda Rae and **George Lozuk**
Venezuela, South America

Contents

PRAYERS
that Changed
HISTORY

1

ABRAHAM

Persistence in Prayer

GENESIS 18:23–33

"Lord, I'm asking one more time."

"Prayer is like opening a sluice between the great ocean and our little channels when the sea gathers itself together and flows in at full tide." With those words Alfred Lord Tennyson described the meaning of prayer for his life.

No doubt prayer has seemed like that to each of us at one time or another. A simple, sincere prayer has seemed to open the gate for a flood of God's blessings.

There have been other times when the answer to prayer did not come immediately, but only after repeated trips to the throne of grace.

Our experience may have been like that of a church in St. Louis which needed an organ. Knowing the philanthropic nature of Andrew Carnegie, the church decided to ask him for the money. At first they sent letters every two weeks, but gradually increased the frequency to one a day. Eight months and eighty-eight letters later they received a check for the amount they had requested. In spite of Carnegie's generous nature, the church had to be persistent.

Abraham had to persist to get what he wanted of God.

If anyone in the Old Testament had a right to expect to receive immediately what he wanted from God, it would be Abraham, the founding father of the Hebrew nation.

For one thing, he had the right attributes. He was personally qualified. He was a man of faith. "He believed in the Lord and he counted it to him for righteousness" (Gen. 15:6). He was faithful in all his actions (18:19). God considered him his friend (Isa. 41:8).

Abraham also had the right attitude for prayer. He was unselfish. He wasn't praying for himself or even for his nephew Lot, but for the whole city. He was humble, saying, "I have taken upon me to speak unto the Lord, which am but dust and ashes." He was reverent, recognizing God's greatness: "Shall not the judge of all the earth do right?"

In addition, Abraham had the right approach to prayer. He was aware of God's presence, for the text says, "Abraham stood yet before the Lord, and Abraham drew near." He knew God's will; God had just revealed his plans to him. He was definite in his prayer. He knew what he wanted.

It has often been suggested that Abraham ceased asking before God quit giving. This might be true. It could be that Abraham thought he had his answer if he had only ten people in mind—Lot, his wife, his two unmarried, and two married daughters, their husbands, and the two messengers.

He had done all the right things to be answered, but he still needed to be persistent in his prayer.

This experience of Abraham is a clear reflection of the

teachings of the Bible. The Bible teaches that we can often expect an immediate answer to our prayers:

"Call unto me and I will answer thee" (Jer. 33:3).

"Before they call, I will answer" (Isa. 65:24).

"Your Father knoweth what things ye have need of, before ye ask him" (Matt. 6:8).

Jesus even instructed his disciples, "When ye pray, use not vain repetitions, as the heathen do" (Matt. 6:7).

But the Bible is also clear that we will often have to persist in prayer. Jesus told two parables, those of the friend at midnight, who persisted in knocking (Luke 11:5–8), and of the importunate widow who kept going back to the judge (Luke 18:1–8). He was making the point "that at all times they ought to pray and not to lose heart" (Luke 18:1, NASB).

Jesus instructed the disciples to "pray always" (Luke 21:36).

Paul told us to "pray without ceasing" (1 Thess. 5:17).

The 120 prayed for ten days in the upper room before the Holy Spirit came.

Cornelius had been praying for some time before the Lord sent Peter.

Paul prayed for three years in Arabia after his conversion experience.

In more recent times Dwight L. Moody prayed for two years for the power of the Holy Spirit to descend on his ministry.

George Mueller, father of orphans and a great man of prayer, prayed for two men for over sixty years. He kept records of his specific requests and records of the answers. One of these two men is supposed to have been converted at the last service Mueller conducted; the other, not until after Mueller's death.

It is clear that, for many things, we will have to persist in prayer. Or, as some used to say, we will have to "pray through."

Why is this true? Why, if the Father knows what we have need of before we ask, must we keep on asking? What is the value of persistent praying?

Delight

Persistent praying is a delight to God. It honors him, just as it honors a loved one to tell him over and over that he is loved.

Sir Walter Raleigh, making a request of Queen Elizabeth, was answered irritably, "Raleigh, when will you leave off begging?" Sir Walter replied, "When Your Majesty leaves off giving." His request was granted.

Abraham kept praying until he received what he wanted. The Lord did not withdraw, did not break off the conversation until Abraham had finished.

God is not wearied with our continued asking. It is a delight to him.

R. A. Torrey writes in his book, *How to Pray,* "God delights in the holy boldness that will not take no for an answer. It is an expression of great faith, and nothing pleases God more than faith."

James tells us that we pray to a God "who giveth to all men liberally and upbraideth not." This means that God will never reproach us or chide us for our asking. On the contrary, it pleases him that we ask, or Jesus would not have taught us to do so.

Persistent praying shows that we know that only God is God. We pray persistently about those things that we cannot or should not handle ourselves. We glorify him by bringing those things to him.

Persistent praying shows that we believe only *he* gives, or, as James writes, "Every good gift and every perfect gift is from above, and cometh down from the Father" (1:17).

When Jesus asked the disciples if they too would turn away, they replied, "To whom shall we go? Thou hast the words of eternal life" (John 6:68). When we continue in prayer, we show that only God gives the good things we need and desire. Persistent praying shows that we have faith in the goodness of God. God is not to be likened to, but contrasted with the unwilling householder and unjust judge in Jesus' parables. We do not wring gifts from an unwilling God, for it is his nature to give.

Demonstration

Not only does our persistence delight God—it also demonstrates our sincerity.

If there is one thing Abraham's prayer reveals, it is earnestness. No one would accuse him of being insincere. The King James Version uses a word in Jesus' parables that could well be used here: importunity. This is the translation of a Greek word which means "shameless persistence." Abraham shamelessly pressed his case, drove his bargain. Nothing would deter him.

Sometimes God tests us to see how sincerely, how keenly, we desire what we ask. Isn't his judgment

proved, when after a time we cease asking without receiving, yet get along as though we had never wanted
anything?

At times God also wishes to increase our desire. Then
when the answer comes, we can more fully appreciate it
and be grateful.

Having to persist in prayer keeps us from praying
carelessly. Just think what would have happened if everything you had prayed for had immediately come to pass!
We are spared the result of many foolish requests by
having to continue in prayer. Having to persist in prayer
drives us to our deepest needs. We will only persevere in
those things that are of utmost importance.

Too many times we pray like little boys who ring
doorbells and then run away. We pray, and when nothing
happens, we say, "Well, it wasn't God's will. I'll just
have to submit to God's will." But, more often than not,
it was God's will for us to persist, not to give up. He
wanted to grant our request if only we had continued.
Praying only one or two times does not show our submis-
siveness but our laziness.

Joash, king of Israel, came to Elisha, the prophet, who
was dying. Joash was concerned about the threat posed
by Syria. Elisha had him take a bow and shoot an arrow
out of the east window. "This is the arrow of the Lord's
deliverance over Syria." Then Elisha told him to strike
the arrows on the floor. Joash did so three times. Elisha
became angry. "Why did you stop?" he asked. "You
should have struck five or six times. Now you will only
defeat Syria in battle three times instead of consuming
them."

Many times we miss the victory or the greater blessing because we do not continue long enough in prayer.

Admiral Peary was victorious in his quest for the North Pole only because he was persistent. He devoted over twenty years to seeking it. The Eskimos told him, "You are like the sun. You always come back." His dominating desire led him to persevere through physical, financial, and natural difficulties. Afterwards he said, "For twenty-four years, sleeping or awake, to place the stars and stripes on the Pole has been my dream."

Should we not seek spiritual victories as earnestly and persistently as Peary sought his geographical one?

Development

Persistence in prayer does something else; it develops our faith.

Remember, Jesus told the disciples that the faith that works miracles "can come forth by nothing but by prayer" (Mark 9:29).

Man becomes physically strong by working continuously. The professional weight lifter is constantly training. Prayer is the gymnasium of the soul. Only through persistent prayer is our faith exercised and strengthened.

Abraham's prayer comes at a crucial point in his life. He had enough faith to believe that God would lead him to a new land and that God would give him the land. But Abraham did not have enough faith to believe God would give him a son. He took matters into his own hands and, through Sarah's handmaiden Hagar, Ishmael was born. God rejected Ishmael in spite of Abraham's pleas. God would do things his way.

His prayer for Sodom and Gomorrah marks a new development in Abraham's character and faith. It is the first intercessory prayer in the Bible. And, it got results. Within a year, Isaac was born.

There are some things God cannot do for us until we are ready ourselves. When we are changed, then God can answer our petitions and grant our desires.

W. E. Sangster tells of an English businessman who had a son named Ted. He intended to send Ted to Cambridge, and Ted was eager to go. But in his late teens Ted seemed to go wild. Finally his father said, "Ted, you can't go to Cambridge. You must enter business with me where I can watch you." Ted was sullen for a week. But then he went to a youth group that was discussing religion. He became interested and soon committed his life to Jesus. His attitude and habits changed. He worked happily. Soon his father told him, "I'm sending you to Cambridge after all. You'll do all right." The father was delighted that his son proved he could go. So our Father delights in giving us the desires of our hearts.

We should persist in prayer so that our faith and character may be developed to the point that God can grant us what we ask.

Delivery

Two reasons for persistent praying are that (1) what we need and desire, only God can give, and (2) persistent praying delivers our desire. Of course, we do not place our trust in prayer, but in God.

Abraham knew that God had passed judgment and only God could spare the city. His prayer was answered!

God did not destroy the righteous with the wicked. As many were spared as would come out of the city.

God has promised to answer persistent prayer. Jesus said, "Ask and ye shall receive. Seek and ye shall find. Knock and it shall be opened." A careful study of the original form of those words shows they could and should be translated, "Keep on asking and ye shall receive. Keep on seeking and ye shall find. Keep on knocking and it shall be opened." The door to the throne room yields to the gentle, persistent knocking of the soul that prays "without ceasing." The way to find God's yes is to refuse to take no for an answer.

We should continue to pray until one of three things happens:

1. God assures us that he has heard our prayer and the answer is on the way;
2. We receive what we ask; or
3. God reveals to us in a definite way that what we ask is not his will for us.

Benjamin Brown tells of the blessing that came through a man who persisted in prayer. His name was Hartwell. While a student at Brown University, Hartwell decided to follow Judson to Burma as a missionary. He was accepted by the Board but failed the physical examination. He was discouraged at first, but relieved when he felt assured from God that he would have a son who would become a missionary.

When the first child came, it was a girl. The second child was also a girl. So were the third, fourth, fifth, and sixth. The seventh was a boy.

As the boy grew, the parents said nothing to him about

becoming a missionary. After graduating from Brown University, he told them he had decided to go to China as a missionary. The father's prayer was answered.

But there is more. That son had four children who all became missionaries. These four children in turn had children who became missionaries. So twelve missionaries came from the family of that one man who persisted in prayer!

What blessings are we missing because we do not persist in prayer? What blessing are we unable to bestow because we have not been persistent in prayer?

God help us to "pray through."

2

MOSES

The Prayer for Pity

NUMBERS 11:10–15

Moses was one of the great intercessors of the Old Testament. God himself paid Moses signal homage when he told Jeremiah that *even if Moses* were to intercede on Judah's behalf, she would not be saved. Even one as powerful as Moses could not save Judah. Regardless of God's decision in that case, the compliment to Moses was the highest of recommendations.

Moses was often called to plead for the people before God. Through most of his lifetime he was in deep distress over his people.

He was at Miriam's bedside, praying for her healing from leprosy (Num. 12:13).

He held the rod of God, a symbol for God's warriors, in the battle against the Amalekites and prayed for Israel's victory (Ex. 17:8–13).

He interceded for them when they went far astray and wildly worshiped the golden calf.

Never again was a prophet to be the agent that Moses was for God's miracles—some of the most amazing miracles in biblical history.

Moses was a man of faith. The writer of Hebrews, discussing and lauding the faith of our fathers, devotes six verses to Abraham's faith; to Moses' he devotes seven. He was the only man who ever lived who spoke with God face-to-face.

Yet, in this passage of Scripture, we see Moses suffering a faith failure.

We know what it is to have a heart attack. We know what it is to suffer a stroke. We know what it means to be stricken with disease. But perhaps we forget what a blow, physically and emotionally, it is to be sick unto death with faith failure. To be spiritually ill is to be devastated, depressed, and without vitality or purpose. And faith failure strikes almost everyone at some time. Past victories through faith do not automatically assure future success. The price of faith, like that of liberty, is constant vigilance.

Not only was Moses a man of unusual faith and a powerful intercessor, but he was also a meek man. The Bible tells us that he was "meek above all the men which were upon the face of the earth" (Num. 12:3). When God approached him, he was hesitant. He reminded God, "O God, I am slow of tongue." Because Moses stuttered, he was reluctant to become a leader of men. He hesitated to go back. His meekness prevented him from defending himself against Miriam and Aaron. Even a strong virtue carries the seed of weakness within.

In these verses we see Moses feeling that he has too much to do, too much responsibility to bear. How many of us have felt that way many times? How many of us have asked, "Why do you treat me like this, Lord? Why

do you place the whole burden upon me and leave me to
bear it alone?'' Or, as *The Living Bible* paraphrases it,
''Why do you pick on me, Lord?'' Why me?

But such a complaint is not the problem, it is only a
symptom of the problem. Let us look at some of the
symptoms Moses was experiencing.

Symptoms

First, Moses was displeased. The people's complaining was evil in his eyes. Their actions and their attitudes
didn't please him. He was angry—not angry for the
Lord's sake, but angry for himself.

Second, he was distressed. The people harassed him.
They made him doubt his acceptability to God. They
criticized him and complained that they hadn't enough
meat for their bellies.

His anger made him defiant. He speaks authoritatively
to God, letting him know in no uncertain terms how he
feels. Emphatically he says over and over, *I, I, I.* ''Why
have *I* not found favor in thy sight? Did *I* conceive all this
people? Did *I* bring them forth. . .?'' No, God, he implies, it was you. Now, you do something about it!

The outcome of this self-pity and anger is Moses'
attitude of defeat. ''If I'm not able to do this alone, if this
is too heavy for me, then just kill me. If I have to do this
all by myself, kill me at once.''

A small child is asked to pick up his toys. Loudly he
wails, ''I have to do EVERYthing! Nobody loves me.''
Moses is complaining thus to God. If you don't love me
any better than this, he says, just do away with me. I
don't care.

Sometimes it seems easier to die than to go on living. Death is less fearful than life, and we haven't the courage or hope to carry us through. Our faith falters, and we wish that death would end it all.

When the POWs returned from Vietnam, they told of the excruciating tortures they had endured. Many said there were times when they no longer wanted to live. Some told of friends who just couldn't hold out and who laid down and died.

For those who came back after a long imprisonment, it was an electrifying moment when they heard the drum-roll and saluted the long-missed flag. But for those who didn't return? Their frustrations and suffering are re-membered and remind us of our own. "Lord, let me out of this terrible situation!" Moses cried.

Have you sometimes felt that way? When you do, what do you do about those feelings of frustration and anger? Perhaps we need to realize that our feelings are outward manifestations of an inner malignancy. The hurt and discouragement and anger are not really the prob-lems, but only the symptoms. To find the cure we must seek the cause. We cannot cure cancer with a Band-Aid.

If people and their actions annoy you, perhaps it is a sign that everything is not right between you and God.

If you feel that people have failed you or let you down, you know how Moses felt when he prayed. You know how discouraged he was.

If it seems that you have more than your share of the load to carry, that you are doing more at home or in the church than anyone else, then you are able to grasp what it was Moses was trying to deal with.

If you feel that your efforts have netted you nothing, then you are feeling something of what Moses felt.

If all these negative feelings are not the root of the problem, what is? Let us see if we can discover the source of the anger.

Source

The real source of Moses' problem lay in three fundamental mistakes he made.

His first mistake was a wrong estimate of the people. At first he thought too highly of them. He expected that, because God had led the people out of Egypt to find the Promised Land, they would be grateful and their behavior would change radically. Such high expectations could only lead to disappointment.

Then, when the people fell in Moses' estimation, he went too far in the other direction and disparaged all of them. When the epidemic of weeping broke out throughout the camp, Moses began to doubt that there was any spiritual quality left in the people. He saw them as unbelievers on whom God's goodness and instruction had been wasted. They would never have enough faith to enter the Promised Land!

But just as his overestimation had led to disappointment, so his underestimation of them led to a surprising discovery. He found that seventy men and women had not worshiped the golden calf. God would pour out his blessing and his Spirit on these few faithful, just as he had shown a despairing Elijah that there were seven thousand faithful.

If we place too much trust in others, we will be

disappointed. This we have already learned from our own experiences in life. By the same token, if we distrust and suspect them too much, we fall into despair and make ourselves miserable.

God can help us if we place our trust in him. Let us seek from God the right estimate of man as did Jesus, who "knew what was in man" (John 2:25).

Not only did Moses mistake what was in man, he also mistook what was in himself. His estimate of his own responsibilities was off target; he took himself too seriously. He felt that he had been carrying the people by himself. But if Moses had been leading them alone, would the people have gotten out of Egypt? Didn't God bring the curse of the plagues?

If only Moses and his powers had been responsible, would the people have been able to cross the Red Sea? Didn't God part the waters?

If it had been up to Moses to provide food and water in the desert wilderness, would the people have survived a single day? Didn't God make available the manna from heaven and the clouds by day and the fire by night?

Like the people, Moses had forgotten God's care of all of them.

Whenever we minimize God's part and maximize our part, we're headed for trouble, anxiety, and despair. If we would stop to realize how little we actually do and how much God does, we would be amazed and ashamed.

That was Moses' biggest mistake: he had a wrong estimate, not only of himself and of the people, but also of God. Moses was not out of favor; God was not out to get him. Moses' heavy burden is certain proof of honor, for in Hebrew there is a simple word which means both "to be heavy" and "to be honored." The greatest men are selected for the greatest missions, the heaviest burdens, and the grandest honors.

At that point in time, Moses' concept of God was too small.

Are we like Moses? We believe that God is powerful enough—at least we believe it theoretically. But do we believe strongly enough that he cares for us?

To underestimate God will surely lead to despair.

Solution

Moses did the right thing. In his despair he took his complaint to the Lord. In doing so, he was more honest than the people who ignored God and tried to solve their problems themselves, or who put all the blame on Moses.

When we complain and blame other people or circumstances for our problems, we are in reality blaming God. Our discontent implies that the world is not well made or well-ordered. It suggests that we could have done a better job. This casts a reflection upon God.

Moses didn't complain *of* God, but *to* God. In doing so he was facing the problem head-on, courageously. He was taking his complaint to the one he thought was responsible. When he did this, he found relief.

Remember the words of songwriter Elisha A. Hoffman?

I must tell Jesus all of my trials;
I cannot bear these burdens alone;
In my distress He kindly will help me;
He ever loves and cares for His own.

When Moses confessed his weakness, he received God's strength.

I believe that this is the secret to intercession for ourselves. If our prayer is full of our helplessness, we receive God's power. Paul made the same discovery. In 1 Corinthians 1:27 he writes, "God hath chosen the weak things of the world to confound the things which are mighty." And God told Paul, "My strength is made perfect in weakness" (2 Cor. 12:9). Therefore Paul could say, "I can do all things through Christ which strengtheneth me" (Phil. 4:13).

Moses found relief in sharing his burden with God. He also found relief in sharing his burden with others. "Not thyself alone," God reminded him. God helps us to bear by telling us to share. Sometimes just telling someone our problems helps us to bear up under them.

Most important is the fact that we can place all our burdens upon Jesus. Didn't he take the greatest burden of all—that of our sin—upon himself and free us for all time on the cross? The Lord laid upon him "the iniquity of us all."

Jesus bears our anxiety and worry: "Let not your heart be troubled," he told the disciples. "You believe in God, believe also in me."

Jesus bears our burdens and trials. "Come unto me, all ye that labour and are heavy laden, and I will give you rest."

Jesus bears our disappointments and griefs.

Let us recognize that most of our complaints are of our own doing, and that by taking them directly to God and laying them on him, we will find a balm in Gilead.

3

JOSHUA

The Posture of Prayer

JOSHUA 5:13–15

Mention the name Joshua and most of us immediately think of the old spiritual, "Joshua Fit the Battle of Jericho." In our mind's eye we see the "walls come a' tumblin' down."

But Joshua's place in holy history is much greater than that one episode.

He was a son of noble parents. His father's name (Nun) means "prosperous, durable."

He was enslaved with the children of Israel in Egypt. Although he may have been a slave outwardly, he was never in bondage inwardly. (Moses found it was easier to get the people out of slavery than to get slavery out of the people.) Joshua was never one of those who wanted to return to the fleshpots of Egypt. Once he had tasted freedom, he looked forward to crossing into the new land.

Joshua was a soldier. Even in the wilderness he led the Israelites to victory over the Amalekites.

He was a subordinate of Moses and became his right-hand man, showing loyalty and devotion.

He was a spy. He and Caleb alone of the twelve spies brought back a true report—that they could conquer the land with God's help.

He was a savior of sorts. His name means "salvation." Moses led the people to the border of the Promised Land, but Joshua led them in to conquer and possess it.

He was a saint. He was filled with the Spirit of God (Deut. 34:9).

He was blessed with the presence of God (Josh. 1:5).

He was a student of the Word of God (Josh. 1:8).

He was obedient to the will of God (Num. 32:12).

Joshua was truly one of the heroes of the Bible. One of the reasons is that he was a mighty man of prayer. All the great men of God—Abraham, Moses, Samuel, Elijah, Isaiah, Jeremiah—have been strong in prayer.

When the disciples asked Jesus how they could obtain so big a faith as to work miracles, he said, "This kind cometh not but by prayer."

Down through the ages the great men of God—Luther, Calvin, Wesley, Edwards, Moody, Billy Graham—have been men of prayer.

Several years ago I had the privilege of being in the headquarters of the Billy Graham Evangelistic Association. Not only was there a huge outlay of offices and a large group of workers, but in the building itself there was also a prayer chapel. The people who worked there came daily to this prayer chapel and prayed for the things they were doing in the name of the Lord.

John Wesley once said that his schedule had become so hectic that he had to increase his prayer time to three hours a day to be able to get everything done.

It seems to be a rule that, if we want to be much *for* God, we must be much *with* God.

The storming of the walls of Jericho is only one of many episodes in the life of Joshua, but it teaches us volumes about his prayer life. First, notice his *observation*.

Observation (v. 13)

Jericho was a huge obstacle blocking the conquest of Canaan. The Israelites dared not leave a fortified city without destroying it for fear its armies attack from behind. Yet, the Jews had neither the experience to seize it nor the equipment for laying siege. Joshua was pondering this problem when he suddenly became aware of a figure standing close to him with a drawn sword in his hand.

There are legends throughout history of men receiving supernatural aid in battle. Greek gods allegedly fought during the Trojan war. In 496 B.C. the mythological gods Castor and Pollux supposedly led the Romans to a strategic victory over the Latins at the Battle of Lake Regillus. Three pillars of a temple built in their honor still stand in Rome.

James became the patron saint of Catholic Spain because, on numerous occasions, he is said to have led them to victory. In A.D. 841 he is said to have led Spain to a strategic victory over the Moslem Moors at Clavijo, slaying sixty thousand Moors himself. He is also said to have aided Cortez in conquering the Aztecs.

Joshua, like those men in the past, sees a man coming. But there is more, for this man is more than a demigod or mythological figure, more than a saint or even an angel.

Who is he?

This mysterious stranger has appeared before in the Scriptures. Elsewhere he is called "the angel" or "the angel of the Lord." He appeared to Abraham when he was sacrificing Isaac, to Hagar when run off by Sarah, to the children of Israel through pillars of fire and smoke, and to Samson's parents before his birth.

Other appearances are similar to this one. It was the angel who appeared to Moses in the burning bush and told him: "Put off thy shoes from thy feet, for the place whereon thou standest is holy ground" (Ex. 3:5).

It was the angel who appeared as a man to Jacob at Peniel and wrestled with him through the night.

It was the angel who appeared to Balaam and his donkey, blocking their path with a drawn sword in his hand.

When the angel speaks to Joshua, the Bible adds, "The Lord said." Who is it that takes on the form of a man and speaks as God? Only Jesus! Here he takes the form of a man temporarily; at Bethlehem he took it on permanently. Also, this "being" allowed Joshua to worship him; an angel would not have done so. So Joshua became aware that the was in the presence of God.

When we pray, are we aware of God's presence? Do we lift up our eyes and see him? Too often we make our prayers vaguely, to no definite person. We just pray about something to someone, somewhere. We pray about nothing in particular, to no one in particular, nowhere in particular.

To pray we should "come boldly unto the throne of grace." There can be no true prayer unless we have a definite awareness of the presence of God. If we want this presence, we must take the time and trouble to seek it. "Ye shall seek me and find me when ye seek me with all your heart."

I have heard many of the saints of God testify that one of the most important aids to their prayer life was a realization of the Lord's presence. God was real to them, and prayer a holy conversation, just as you and I talk to those on earth we love. Some designate a chair as the Lord's chair and talk to him as if he were sitting there.

When you pray, make sure that the Lord is there.

Obeisance (v. 14)

At a meeting of a literary society in London, someone raised the question, "What would we do if Shakespeare should walk into the room?"

One person answered, "We would all rise to our feet and applaud and shout his genius."

Then someone else asked, "What would we do if Jesus Christ should walk into the room?" Quietly Charles Lamb replied, "We would fall to our knees and bow and cry, 'My Lord and my God.' "

When Joshua recognized this being as divine, he fell down before him with his face to the ground just as one day "every knee shall bow and every tongue confess that Jesus is Lord" (see Phil. 2:10–11). If we really had a sense of God's presence, would not we too fall on our knees and bow down? To do so is obeisance.

One of the best practices to cultivate in praying is to kneel. Before God, we stand tallest when we are on our knees. This posture is conducive to prayer. We should copy Joshua's posture—bended knee and bowed head.

There are postures not conducive to prayer, such as lying in bed. The temptation is too great to fall asleep, instead of to prevail in prayer. Would you dare fall asleep while talking to the President or a king?

There are other bad postures, such as sitting in front of the television set or bending over a golf club. It is possible to pray at these times, but difficult. Most of us need all the help in prayer we can get.

Getting on our knees is probably the best posture because it leads to a right attitude. We should be humbled and reverent, both physically and spiritually.

The Pharisee stood upright and was proud in prayer. The publican bowed and humbled himself. Jesus said God accepted the publican's prayer.

One author wrote, "Reverence is the anteroom which leads into the audience chamber of the King."

I remember one occasion when a layman and I went to visit a friend of ours whose wife was a member of our church. We had visited him many times before, but we were now in a revival and felt compelled to see him again. He was out in the fields on his tractor. When he reached the end of a row, he stopped and talked to us. He was kind and courteous, but he did not get off nor cut off the engine; and we had difficulty hearing over it. I said, "Let's pray," and when I did, two things happened. The layman, who was a very wealthy man, immediately sank to his knees in the dirt in his fine suit. No sooner had he dropped there than the man cut off his tractor and it grew quiet. We prayed and urged him to come to the service. The only words he uttered were, "What time is the service tonight?'' We told him, and went on our way.

That evening his uncle, a new Christian, was waiting at the church to ask how we came out. We told him we weren't sure, and related what had happened. The uncle said, ''Preacher, the next time, get him down on his knees; I became a Christian when I got on my knees.''

Reverence and humility before God—obeisance—are the first steps in winning the battle.

When Abraham fell on his face, God talked to him (Gen. 17:3). Daniel was on his face when the Lord spoke to him (Dan. 10:9). Joshua said, ''What saith my lord unto his servant?'' In other words, ''What do you want, Lord?'' Those who have a humble heart will also have an open ear.

If we would hear God speak, we must humbly wait before him. It is said that no man ever went away from Jesus empty except the man who was full of himself. ''For God resisteth the proud but giveth grace to the humble. Humble yourselves therefore under the mighty hand of God, that he may exalt you in due time'' (1 Pet. 5:5–6).

Obedience (v. 15)

When God speaks to us, we must be ready to obey!

For Joshua, humility led to reverence and reverence to obedience. This is a natural sequence for all of us. The reason there is so little obedience to Christ is that there is so little love for him.

Have you ever wondered why the disciples were willing to leave their families and possessions to go to strange lands, only to be tortured and killed for preaching the good news? Paul gives us the answer, "The love of Christ constraineth us." This is the only true motive for service.

Jesus said, "If ye love me, keep my commandments." Note that the Lord said, "As captain . . . I am come." The word *captain* literally means "chief ruler." The Lord does not come as a private but as the general. He is not our servant but our master. He is not our helper; he is our leader.

Someone said to Lincoln during the days of the Civil War, "Let us pray that God be on our side." Lincoln replied, "Let us pray that we be on God's side." God does not change sides.

Jesus said, "He that is not for us is against us." It is up to us to choose to be on his side. The Lord does not choose sides.

Joshua's obedience is aptly summed up in the phrase, "And Joshua did so." Later we find this recorded: "As the Lord commanded Moses his servant, so did Moses command Joshua, and so did Joshua; he left nothing undone of all that the Lord commanded Moses" (Josh. 11:15).

Joshua is a perfect example of complete obedience because he always knew who was in command: not himself, but the Lord.

How do we measure up to this example? Most of us want to obey; we intend to, but we don't. We are like the artist who was called the biggest dreamer in Paris. In his attic studio every inch of the ceiling and walls was covered with sketches of angels, sunsets, trees, castles, clouds, persons. Even the floor had sketches on it.

Thousands of sketches, none of them complete. Few of them ever made their way to the canvas. Artists with one tenth the imagination had painted ten times as much. He did not have the ability to complete the job.

For many, Christianity is just a dream, a vision, an incomplete sketch, because they've never become obedient. Joshua had to do some unreasonable things. He had to march his men around Jericho carrying pitchers. Jesus warned that we also would have to do unreasonable deeds, like "lose your life and find it." Like "love your enemies." Like "turn the other cheek."

We cannot choose which commands we will obey and which we won't. In the army, that would lead to court-martial. We must obey them all.

Jesus said, "Not everyone that saith unto me, Lord, Lord, shall enter into the kingdom of heaven; but he that doeth the will of my Father which is in heaven" (Matt. 7:21).

Isn't this the posture of prayer? To lift up our eyes to seek his presence, to fall on our faces humbly and reverently before him, and to throw our lives into the doing of the tasks he gives us?

Let the record say of us as it said of Joshua, "And he did so."

4

ELIJAH

The Prayer for Priority

1 KINGS 18:17–39

Why some playwright has not written a drama out of this passage of Scripture, I have never really understood. It is one of the most unusual in all of God's Word. As I read it I feel like that early English divine who said, "Me thinks I would like to have been there." Yet had I been there, I wonder if my faith or my heart would have stood it!

"When Ahab saw Elijah, Ahab said to him, 'Is it you, you troubler of Israel?' And he answered, 'I have not troubled Israel; but you have, . . . because you have forsaken the commandments of the Lord and followed the Baals. Now, therefore, send and gather all Israel to me at Mount Carmel, and the four hundred and fifty prophets of Baal and the four hundred prophets of Asherah.' . . . So Ahab sent to all the people of Israel, and gathered the prophets together at Mount Carmel. And Elijah said, . . . 'If the Lord is God, follow him; but if Baal, then follow him' " (1 Kings 18:17–39, RSV).

Elijah then had two bulls cut in pieces and lay the pieces on the wood of the altar. He ordered the followers of Baal to call upon their god for fire. When they got no answer, he called his people together and had them pour water over the wood, drenching it three times. And then he prayed.

We can envision three groups gathered around. The first is Ahab's hundreds, there in number and splendor. You can just imagine these crowds who have been ordered, perhaps paid, to be there. They have the king on their side. They are government-sponsored. Everything is going their way.

The second group is a halting, wavering crowd of in-betweens, not sure where they stand. They are tense, uncertain how the contest will turn out and ready to spring to the winning side. These are a difficult bunch to count on.

Then there is God's side—as usual, a minority. As far as we know, Elijah stands alone, bold and aggressive like Peter and John, yet humble. Yet he is not alone, anymore than any servant of God has ever stood alone.

Elijah's philosophy could be called a "philosophy of priority." It was a philosophy of two parts—the principle and the practice. The principle was, If God be God, so be it! The practice: If God be God, let us follow him! We are not only to think, but also to serve.

When God is ready, he chooses a man, a man of the hour, the time, the century. We need a man like Elijah now!

Billy Graham remarked that the same century that produced the novel *Tom Jones* in England also produced the man John Wesley. Wesley had been barred from the churches of England. He became a circuit-rider preacher.

At the same time, George Whitefield had begun preaching at an abandoned race track in Bristol. Wesley, without a church building to preach in, joined with him. That was the beginning of the great open-air revivals, when men left the church buildings to hear the word of God preached. As a result, God sent revival to England and saved her from a possible revolution like the bloody one through which France went.

When will America have a man of prayer, a man of the century to lead it to prayer, to revival?

When the time had fully come, God chose Elijah to challenge the hordes of hell. Would that we would hear and respond to such a challenge!

The Protest

Elijah was a quiet man. He didn't carry a sword like Peter, who severed the ear from the soldier's head, or the hatchet of Francis Willard, who chopped up saloons. But he believed in prayer as did John Knox, who with his praying shook Mary, Queen of Scots, half off the throne.

Few people seek prayer from the church anymore. Many come for groceries, for clothes, for shelter, for friendship. Few come for prayer. We seem to think we don't need prayer anymore. It has become a ritual or a pastime. But prayer is a weapon, a source of power much stronger than the budgets and programs we put our faith in.

Peter told the beggar, "Silver and gold have I none, but such as I have, give I thee." Such as we have! That is all God asks, and each of us *can* pray.

To disregard the power of prayer is to make God

noneffective in our lives. To ignore him is to dethrone him. Elijah wanted the true God of the Commandments to be honored. Do you suppose that someday they will read of the day they called a prayer meeting in the twentieth century to awaken the Christian God?

God still has the power, but who has the heart or the faith for such an experience? The Bible says, "At the name of Jesus, every knee shall bow," but I wonder whether it will be conscience or calamity that calls us to our knees?

Priority time has come; we must set goals. If we seek a purpose, we shall find it.

Elijah protested, "God will be God." God will be God! Every man, whether he is behind a pulpit or a plow, a desk or a counter, will have to decide whether God is going to be God in his life, or whether something, or someone else will sit on the throne.

The Preparation

Protest wasn't enough. There had to be something more positive to go along with that. There had to be preparation.

Elijah was prepared. He had rested. God had been waiting on him.

Elijah gave Ahab and his people the edge. He let them pray first.

He let them pray longer.

He let them say all they wanted to say.

He prodded and poked. "Pray louder!" he jeered. "Perhaps Baal is asleep, or on vacation!" They wore themselves out. They did everything they could think of and still Baal was silent. He waited until they had had enough, until they gave up hope.

Perhaps that is the only time God will be heard—when the rest of our gods have fallen aside and we realize they won't hold up in a crisis. Then God is ready. Elijah was ready. When they knew they couldn't help themselves, they were ready to throw in the towel.

Can you picture the scene as Elijah, his confidence returning, walked around the high priests, daring them, challenging them, waiting, waiting, waiting? He had found peace; he knew he was going to win; he knew God was on his side and the victory was his.

Perhaps it would have scared the people to death if the fire had fallen for them! Surely this wasn't the first time they had prayed to Baal and nothing had happened. They had been praying to Baal all their lives and nothing had happened. Why did they expect it now? They probably didn't. Their faith in Baal was no greater than their faith in God. They didn't believe—they just hoped that maybe. . . . They were going through a ritual, and hoping.

Are we?

The Plea

After Elijah set his priorities, found his purpose, and prepared, he pled with God in prayer. The Bible doesn't tell us whether he lay prostrate on the ground, or knelt, or stood looking heavenward. But we do know that he was facing God. And he said, "Lord, I am your servant. The time is now; reveal yourself and we will get things straightened out. God will be God, and Baal will be Baal, a mere graven image.''

You know what happened; it is a matter of history. What we don't know is whether it could happen again in our time.

"Let the fire fall!"

Have you ever stood in Yosemite National Park at the floor of the valley where the campgrounds are, and watched the fire fall? People from every state in the union and from all over the world used to go there to see this event. Up on the mountaintop, high above, a bundle of wood is put together. It is then set afire to smolder all day, and as evening falls, begins to burn brightly. When the crowd has gathered, at the appointed time someone cries, "Let the fire fall!" and the bundle comes tumbling down. As I watched, a gawky-eyed tourist, my heart rose in my throat.

When will our hearts swell with the real fire? When will the fire fall for us? It will fall for us when we put God back on his throne and make him the priority of our lives.

It will fall when we serve him with gladness rather than sadness.

It will fall when we forget personal safety or reputation and risk all for him.

It will fall when we want it to and believe that it will.

A foreigner greatly influenced by John Wesley bowed at his tomb and was overheard to say, "Do it again, Lord, do it again!"

Let that be our prayer: "Let the fire fall again, Lord, now!"

5

HEZEKIAH

The Prayer for Preservation

2 KINGS 20:1–11

"Lord, please don't let me die."

Hezekiah's prayer was, "Lord, let me live and not die." This prayer is 2,600 years old, yet it is as new today as it was then. Thousands doubtlessly pray that same prayer daily in hospitals and homes across the land. Perhaps you have prayed it yourself. Maybe you have prayed it for your loved ones. Maybe you will pray it in the future.

After his defeat in the 1960 presidential election, Richard Nixon wrote a book entitled *Six Crises*. Hezekiah was head of state in his day, and he could have written a book called *Four Crises*.

What were the crises Hezekiah faced?

First, he faced the crisis of choice. Early in his kingship he chose to forsake the idols of his fathers. He tore down the idols and rebuilt the city of God. Certainly this was no easy thing to do.

Second, he faced the crisis of invasion. The marauding Assyrians came right to the walls of Jerusalem and threatened to enter the city and destroy it. Had it not been for the power of prayer, Judah might have been conquered.

Third, Hezekiah faced the crisis of prosperity. Foolishly, he displayed all his personal wealth and the treasures of his kingdom and his people before a delegation from Babylon. Because of vanity he revealed to his enemies his strengths and weaknesses.

Finally, Hezekiah faced the most personal crisis of all: the crisis of death. What message of encouragement may we find from the way Hezekiah faced death?

Message of the Prophet (v. 1)

When Isaiah the prophet approached Hezekiah, he told him, "Thus saith the Lord." Isaiah was saying, There's no need to call in another specialist. No other opinion is sought. The ultimate authority has spoken; you will die. Heed his words.

Isaiah told him, "Thou shalt die and not live." Note the severity of the announcement. How abrupt! How emphatic! How disturbing! How unconditional! No words of comfort from the prophet of God. There seemed to be no way out. "The Lord has spoken," he added, and Hezekiah did not question the verdict or the authority.

Then Isaiah said, "Set thine house in order." Issue orders to your household, he was saying. Make preparations. Hezekiah had made no preparations for death, even though both his father and his grandfather had died at an early age.

Few of us get a warning like Hezekiah's. For most of us death comes without warning and disrupts the normal pattern of life. It comes "as a thief in the night," at an hour when we think not.

If we did have warning, what would our reaction be? feverish preparations? fearful paralysis? fierce profanity? Would we question, Why me, Lord? Why me?

In a sense we have all been warned. The Bible says, "It is appointed unto man once to die and after that the judgment." Knowing this, why do we run, sticking our heads into the ground like ostriches as if to say, "Not I, Lord, not I"?

What is your reaction to the light you have? For most of us it is foolish procrastination. Those of us who are wise will set our houses in order.

Motive of the Prayer (vv. 2–3)

The Scriptures tell us that when Isaiah had given him the pronouncement, Hezekiah "turned his face to the wall." He needed some uninterrupted time with God. He recognized that Isaiah was a man of God, and as a man of God himself he did not question the judgment. He knew that if God sent Isaiah to deliver the message, the message was true. So he turned to God in his time of trouble. He prayed, interceding for himself.

Many of us in times of trouble tend to blame God. We turn to leisure activities to get our minds off our problems. We turn to drink. We turn to psychiatrists, or turn inward, or turn away. But rather than be embittered, this man turned to God in his moment of despair.

Hezekiah wanted to live. There were a number of reasons he might have wanted so badly to live.

There was the rational reason. He was too young to die. He was probably only about thirty-nine years of age.

There was the national reason. Assyria was threatening

to attack and might, even at that moment, have the city surrounded. The nation needed its leader.

There was the religious reason. He had begun some reforms and needed time to complete them.

There was the familial reason. He had no heir, no son to replace him on the throne.

But Hezekiah gave none of these reasons for wanting to live. He gave a selfish reason. He prayed, "Lord, I'm too good to die. I have walked in truth and have done what is good in your sight. I don't deserve to die."

He did not want to die, and Hezekiah had more reason to be afraid than do we, who have the message of the gospel. For Hezekiah the future was uncertain; the way was dark. What lay beyond death wasn't clear. He had no assurance of eternal life. To him death was not only fatal but also final. What a difference knowledge of Christ makes!

We can be encouraged by Hezekiah's experience. We can see that, though a variety of motives underlies our prayers, God can and does answer them, even when they are selfish. However, it might be well to take care in our prayers, lest we get what we ask for. Hezekiah asked to live. His prayer, for whatever reason, was answered, and he lived to bear a son who became the most evil ruler in Judah's history.

Miracle of the Poultice (vv. 4–11)

Hezekiah based his plea on his past goodness; God based his answer on Hezekiah's prayer and tears.

How quickly the answer came! No sooner had Isaiah left the room than God spoke to him and said, "Go back and tell Hezekiah he will live another fifteen years." The healing was not instantaneous, but the assurance of an affirmative answer came immediately. The miracle was the work of God. God told Isaiah to put a lump of figs on the boil, and the poultice healed the sore. And with the healing came the assurance that, even as God had been with Moses, so was he with Hezekiah. God who was Elohim (the God of might and majesty), Yahweh (the One who was, is, and will be), and the God of David was the same yesterday, is today, and will be forever.

God sees, God hears, God acts; and with him all things are possible. Is anything too hard for the Lord? God had asked that question of Abraham and Sarah. Jesus had the answer: "With God all things are possible."

Do we believe that God can do all things? Intellectually we understand that nothing is too hard for God. But emotionally we doubt his ability to change lives and circumstances. We don't bother to ask.

God does not work alone. He always uses human agents. That is why he required the prayer and the poultice. He asked for faith and figs in order to deliver the miracle.

God often uses human instruments for heavenly needs. Are we available when help is needed?

Meaning of the Postponement (v. 6)

Men confronted by death often have a greater understanding of life. So it was with Hezekiah. According to Isaiah, he celebrated his recovery by composing a psalm. In it he spoke about the things by which men live.

When a man faces death, whether real, imagined, or

vicarious, he learns what is really important to him. He discovers what his priorities are.

It is said that, as P. T. Barnum of Barnum and Bailey Circus lay on his deathbed, his last words were, "What were the day's receipts?"

All of us live by something—convictions, theories, or ideas that govern our lives. It is these things that comfort and inspire. Some of us seek comfort in the material, finding satisfaction in things. Some of us seek emotional thrills, momentary pleasures that have a way of slipping away. Some of us seek intellectual fulfillment, as though filled heads would mean filled hearts. Some of us find satisfaction in worship and service to others. Our comforts are spiritual.

What are your comforts? What principles do you live by? Are you ready to face death now? Only when you're ready to die will you be really ready to live. Only the spiritual values will pass the test of death.

A young woman praying for her uncle's conversion finally persuaded him to go with her to church. To her dismay the minister preached from Genesis 5, a chapter on genealogy. As they left the church she felt terribly disappointed that the sermon had not been on salvation. She wept, thinking that all her prayers had been for nought. But later that evening her uncle accepted Christ. He had heard the phrase "and he died" repeated eight times in the Scripture passage, and the words haunted him. As he came face to face with the reality of death, he turned to Christ for salvation. As he prepared for death, he began to live.

Do you have some preparations to make?

6

HANNAH

The Prayer of Pledge

1 SAMUEL 1:9–18

We hear the rapture of a soul poured out to God as we listen to the prayer of Hannah: "Lord, if you will . . . I will." Hers is a prayer of pledge.

Over four million girls in the United States are named after Mary of the Bible. She is clearly the most favored of women. Yet Mary probably received inspiration from Hannah who, in the Old Testament, personifies ideal motherhood.

Look at her son Samuel. Wasn't every great man in the Bible influenced by some woman?

Abraham had his Sarah.

Isaac had his Rachel.

Samson had his Delilah, and Ahab his Jezebel!

Samuel, the first great prophet since Moses, had Hannah.

The proof of motherhood is in the children, and Samuel is one of the most outstanding men of the Old Testament. Yet Hannah almost was not a mother. Had the Lord not favored her, she would have borne no children. But that is the very meaning of her name—"favored."

Hannah has been called the model mother of the Old Testament. The Bible speaks of her sorrow, her supplication, her sacrifice. Let us look at her sorrow.

Sorrow (vv. 1–10)

Hannah had a husband and a house, but she didn't have a home. In this day of easy abortion, population explosion, and countless unwanted children, it is perhaps hard for us to understand the deep, genuine sorrow of this Jewish mother. She bore the stigma of being barren, a heavy burden for any Jewish woman. She was taunted by her husband's other wife—taunted as were Sarah and Rachel. Elkanah, her husband, tried to console her, but she wept bitterly. She was anguished, deeply distressed. Even God seemed deaf to her weeping.

Because Hannah was sorrow-stricken, she kept asking God why. Why, God, why?

Like Hannah, we sometimes ask, Why does God allow us to get into such difficult situations? Why does he seem to ignore us?

Perhaps he is preparing us. He needed a man like Samuel, so he made a mother.

Perhaps he is using us. He used Hannah's son to bless a nation.

Perhaps he has something better in mind. Samuel became famous and Hannah bore five more children.

Heavy burdens can be the most enriching events in our lives. Consider the grandfather clock with its heavy pendulum. If it did not bear that pendulum, time would cease to be told. If we bear no burdens, perhaps we do not experience life as deeply and fully as we might. Perhaps

God's will is not being done in our lives.

Supplication (vv. 11–18)

Hannah was sorrow-stricken before God. In pouring out her soul before him, she felt she was taking the last step. She came before the altar with fear and trembling. Her lips moved silently in desperation. She knew that this was her last resort, and she was willing to do anything God wanted her to do so that her prayer might be answered. Her supplication became a giving of self.

When mothers come to the place that they are willing to do anything God wishes them to do, their prayers will be answered. The answer may not be immediate; it may not be what the mother prayed for. But I am convinced that a prayer persistently offered will not go unheard.

Perhaps the reason we don't get through to God sometimes is that we don't want to badly enough.

An older man showed a younger man what it means to want something badly. He led him to the water and pushed the young man's head under. He held him there until the man wanted to breathe so badly that he struggled with all his might. The older man explained, "That is how intense all your desires should be. And when you want something as badly as you wanted breath just now, you will have it."

When praying becomes synonymous with breathing—when our very breath is a prayer of supplication—then surely God will hear us.

Hannah didn't utter vague generalities. She didn't pray aimlessly or tritely or thoughtlessly. She prayed no rote prayer. She didn't pray to impress Eli, or because her husband expected her to. She prayed specifically. She knew what she wanted and she asked for it, fervently, humbly, but with determination.

Vague or guilty prayers will not change people or nations; Hannah expected results. When Eli assured her that God was going to answer her prayer, she believed him. She was still barren, but she believed him; and she prayed believing that she would be heard.

When we pray, do we believe? Do we think that God is hearing our prayer? Do we know that he will answer?

Hannah knew. Eli assured her and she believed. And when her supplication was answered, she sang praises to God for all he had done for her.

Sacrifice (vv. 11,19–28)

What joy there must have been when Hannah's prayer was answered! Her joy is evident in her song. Yet, there was some sadness, too.

Hannah prayed, "Lord, if you will . . . I will. If you will give me a child, I will give him to you. I will lend him to you all the days of his life. I will not cut his hair, and the traditions of his father will be upheld. He shall learn in the temple."

Hannah made a solemn pledge before God. She made it from the depths of her own soul. She asked God for a son, and she named him Samuel, which means "ask of the Lord." And now that she had promised, she must keep her word. To Hannah a promise meant something. To her a promise was a debt unpaid. She had asked for a son and God had given her a son, and now she must give him back. Surely there was a little sorrow mingled with

her joy as she realized the sacrifice that must be made.
She might have wished that she could give her own life
rather than give up her son. To see him leave home at a
young age and go to the temple was hard for a mother
with a long-awaited firstborn. But she had made a vow
before God, and in Israel a vow was a pledge that must be
fulfilled. Israel needed a leader more than this mother
needed her son.

People in crises often make promises they don't mean.
In domestic difficulties, in times of ill health or financial
struggles we promise all kinds of things to God, if only
he will see us through this one time. Only God knows
how many promises have been made and broken because
no one but God and us have lived to see the proof.

Is it any wonder that the man Samuel knew how to
pray? Is it any wonder that he became a prophet of God
and a leader of men? Is it any wonder that, as a small
boy, he heard the voice of God and answered, "Speak,
Lord, for thy servant heareth"? With a mother like Hannah to pray for him all the days of his life, is it any
wonder that he became one of the great men of Israel?

Hannah gave up the most treasured thing in her life. If
she had not made her sacrifice, her son might not have
heard the voice of God that night. If no sacrifices are
made, will your children learn to pray?

If no prayers are uttered in your home, will your
children know God?

If no vows are made and kept, will your children learn
the meaning of a promise?

Hannah knew nothing of Mother's Day, but she ex-
perienced it nonetheless. To Hannah Mother's Day was

that one day in the year when she brought a new coat to Samuel at the temple. She sacrificed all year, working on the coat, so that he could have a new one each year to wear under his garments in the tabernacle.

It is Mother's Day in a home when a child comes to know God.

It is Mother's Day when a mother hears her children pray.

It is Mother's Day when children walk in fear of the Lord.

Have we done as Hannah? Have we laid our all on the altar? It is never too late for God to hear our prayer.

7

SAMUEL

The Partner in Prayer

1 SAMUEL 12:16–25

The story of Samuel raises the question, "What should I pray for?" or "Why should I pray for you?"

Samuel was the prophet of God. He had been the ruler of Israel, the last of the judges to rule. Now all around him other nations were emerging. In that period of growth and change, other countries were beginning to inaugurate and crown kings. Soon the people of Israel were asking each other, Why should we remain the only people different? Why should we be the only ones who don't have a king? They convinced themselves that, militarily speaking, they would be better off with a king than they would with a prophet.

So the day came when they went to Samuel and asked him to step down. He did. He gave them what they asked. But when circumstances did not go as they wanted, they began to see the folly of their choice. So they sought out Samuel, who was residing somewhere in retirement, letting them have their way. They came to him and said, "Samuel, we don't have the right to ask you, but please pray for us." In greatness and in righteousness he replied, "I have never ceased to pray for you." He had been their silent partner in prayer all along.

Have you driven across the plains where you could see further and yet see less? Have you traveled the desert in biblical places and seen the great void, the great waste, not even a mirage in sight to add to the scenery? Have you passed through a valley shaded by mountains on either side?

Well, Samuel was one of the mountaineers of God. Clovis Chappell wrote of this man that the landscape of biblical history was monotonously flat until Samuel came on the scene. Some of us will live, die, be buried, and forgotten and the world may not be much better or worse for our living and dying. But the whole nation of Israel recognized its dependence upon Samuel; they knew that one man, Samuel, could make a difference. He was the kind of man who changes the course of human history.

Yet, it seems odd that a man who almost was not born turned out to be so important in Israel's history. Hannah prayed and pled and promised God that her child would belong to him. And when God answered her prayer, she kept her word. She made him a child of prayer and a servant of God.

You will recall how Hannah made Samuel a coat and took him to the great Eli down at the temple. It was not an abandonment, but a dedication of his life as she had promised. He came to the temple early in life.

Incessant

God tried to speak to Samuel. At first Samuel did not know how to discern the will of God. He did not recognize the voice. The boy woke Eli more than once, asking, "Did you call?" Finally the wise teacher said to him, "If you hear the voice again, say, Speak, for thy servant heareth." Samuel learned early, not *if* thou prayest, but *when* thou prayest. He learned early to listen in prayer.

When did you first really hear the voice of God? It may not have been audible to your ears, but it certainly was to your heart and mind. You knew in unmistakable fashion that this insistent voice of God was speaking to you. I hope that you still hear the voice, and that you listen to it. It is never easy to know fully the voice of God.

Amy Bolding, who has written many devotional books, says that the first time she remembers God speaking to her was in her favorite place for prayer—behind the old organ of the little one-room church of her early childhood. That was not an unusual place for boys and girls to be because they had to take turns pumping the organ. In that little corner, out of sight, she heard the insistent voice of God speaking to her heart.

It is not always easy to hear the voice of God amid the tumult of our lives. We attribute many things to God that aren't related to God at all. Everything that we blame on God, calling it "his will," isn't his doing. Everything we blame on the devil isn't his doing, either. Some of it is just our doing, and we are hunting for a scapegoat.

It is tragic for a member or a preacher to hear only the voice of the church and suppose that it must be the will of God. It is equally tragic for a member not to hear the voice of the church or a committee. For God speaks in many ways, and one way is through the leadership of the Holy Spirit through other mortals. God uses individuals.

The insistent voice of God called Samuel that he might be used.

Intercession

Jesus instructed his disciples, not "*if* you pray," but "*when* you pray." It goes without saying that the Christian should want to commune with the Father as much as a child wants to commune with his earthly father. Something is wrong when there is no communication. There is nothing worse than a deathly silence in the house of God or in the house of man. That kind of silence is chilling.

Now, intercessory prayer is prayer that cares. I heard someone purposely change the words of the hymn from "Sweet hour of prayer" to "Sweet hour of care." Prayer is not prayer unless there is caring.

Prayer is not prayer unless there is sharing. Remember the four men who brought the cripple to Jesus?

Prayer is not prayer unless there is bearing of one another's burdens. Remember the centurion who believed that his daughter would be healed? He carried her burden to Jesus.

Of all the prayers that man might pray, the noblest besides the prayer of adoration is the prayer for someone else, the intercessory prayer. When Samuel was told he was no longer needed in public service, he retired to private prayer. Anyone anywhere can pray in secret.

When the people came to Samuel and said, "Pray for us," did Samuel say, "I would not sin against you"? No. He said, "I would not sin against the Lord in ceasing to pray for you. I have never quit." The people were his responsibility whether he was in leadership or not. He felt that he would be sinning before God if he quit praying for them. It is a sin *not* to pray for others.

It was Samuel's job to intercede for the people. And he refused to be fired from the job to which God had called him. He may not have been praying publicly for them, but privately he had continued to speak on their behalf. He did not want to sin against God. He recognized that all sin is first against God.

Samuel could have been highly indignant at his people's request. Most of us would have been. But there is no place for this kind of pride in the life of a Christian. A Christian has responsibilities in prayer. Samuel won the victory on his knees.

The sin of prayerlessness is the worst sin of the saints of God in the church today! Are you a sinner? How long has it been since you prayed for anyone? How long since you said other than a memorized prayer that God bless the sick and sorrowing? The sick and sorrowing need our prayers, but not in memorized fashion.

There are two kinds of sin—the sin of omission and the sin of commission. The sin of commission is doing what I know to be wrong. The sin of omission is *not* doing what I know to be right. James put it this way: "He that knoweth to do good and doeth it not, to him it is sin." God has given you the power, not only to change your life, but also the lives of your families, your church, and your nation.

Remember the open-air revival in England? Perhaps we could start a carpet revival in America if we were willing to pay the price!

The symbol of Christianity is not a mere cross or a

crucifix but a torn veil between the holy of holies and that man who is a priest before God. What made the difference between Judaism and Christianity was when the veil was torn in two and no longer could someone else bear the responsibility for our sins.

A little child traveled alone from Scotland to London to have a series of operations for her twisted body. Because of the distance, she had to leave her family behind. A sympathetic nurse tried to condition the child to the routine of the hospital, introducing her to this doctor and that nurse. When everything was explained, the nurse asked, "Do you have any questions?" The child answered, "Yes. Who is going to pray for me?"

We may be able to take care of all the other arrangements, but if we fail in our prayer life for others, then we have indeed failed.

Individual

I would not dare pray for less than the whole world. I would not dare try to restrict my prayer before God and say, "Lord, this only includes people of certain races. I am not interested in praying for anybody else." We can't tell God who he is supposed to save.

Any shepherd dies a bit when his sheep die. Samuel was that kind of shepherd. When his people hurt, he hurt; when his people rejoiced, he rejoiced. He wept over their misfortune.

The greatest test of Samuel's prayer life was in his prayers for individuals. He had prayed for Saul until finally the voice of God spoke to him and told him to give Saul up. Samuel's attitude was right. He cared and was humble before God. He grew in relationship with God.

How long should we pray for people? How long should we visit people? How long should we witness to people? How long should we strive for people? Until God tells us it is enough. Any less won't do. Intercessory prayer is a showing of faith.

How great is your faith?

8

GIDEON

The Prayer for Proof

JUDGES 6:12–17

The writer of Hebrews said, "What more shall I say? For time would fail me to tell of Gideon" (11:32). If there wasn't enough time for the writer of Hebrews who wrote the roll call of the ages and the faith, surely there isn't enough time for us.

Indeed, Gideon is the thrilling story of how God in his divine purpose finds men, calls men, and uses men—to the happiness of both. His story is the result of God's search for a man willing to give himself to full-time Christian service. It is the story of Gideon's response to God's will for his life. It is something that can happen to each of us.

God's appearance to us may not be as dramatic as it was to Gideon. It may not be as sudden or as blinding as was the light to Saul on the way to Damascus.

It may be less sensational.

It could come quietly from the persistent prayers of a nominating committee.

It could come in the concern of a staff for its pastor.

It could come through the kind gesture of some interested friend, or through the sudden touch of a messenger from the Lord.

Or, it could come from the depths of our own hearts as we seek God's will and respond to it in our own lives.

God's call is not always expected. Sometimes we cannot explain why God works as he does, performing his miracles in mysterious ways. Remember the call of God to Samuel as a child? Remember how God chose David, the shepherd boy, the least likely to serve? Remember his urgent call to Elijah at Ahab's court? Remember the call he gave Isaiah at the Temple? Remember how he approached the stuttering Moses at the burning bush? Remember the call of his own Son to a cross on Calvary's hill between two thieves? God works in wondrous ways.

Gideon was called at a time of national distress, a time when the people did not honor God. He was not called to be a judge but rather to be a prophet, a leader, a man of God.

One of our greatest problems today—a time much like Gideon's—is that many of us have not found ourselves. We have no purpose, no goals. We are not interested in God's will for our lives. We go around in circles rather than do what is purposeful in the mind of God.

He Calls the Courageous

God calls men who are courageous.

Judges 6:12 says, "The Lord is with thee, thou mighty man of valour." Those were strange words to Gideon's ears. He felt anything but courage. But the clue comes in verse 14, where God tells him, "Go in this might of

yours and deliver Israel . . . ; do not I send you?"
(RSV). When a man is sure of his calling, when he is
positive of the presence of God, then he is not fearful of
the multitudes and the hordes of hell cannot stop him.

Gideon did not want to rush out. He was a timid man.
He was waiting to find God's way for his life. He needed
a sign. And when he got it, suddenly he had the courage
to be a prophet instead of a puppet, and he reached up.

God saw Gideon both as he was and as he could be.
With divine insight, God looked at the finished product,
while you and I look only at the raw material.

God looks at us in the same way he looked at Gideon.
He sees what we are now and what we could be by his
grace.

God's will for Gideon was not unique or there would
be no purpose in this message. His message was univer-
sal. He wanted to restore a lost faith in Israel. He wanted
to restore freedom to God's people. His will for Gideon's
life is his will for all men's lives—that they find the will
of God and do it.

He Calls the Confused

He was a man of courage, but close to the raw courage
was admitted confusion. He raised a question that all of
us have raised. "If the Lord is with us, why then is all
this befallen us?"

Have you ever asked that? Have you ever wondered it?
You may not have said it aloud, but maybe in the secret
caves of your mind those subconscious thoughts have
been hidden away. "Lord, it seems to me that you are
making a mess of this thing. If you are with me and I am

doing your will and the right thing, will you please explain the circumstances that are going on?"

Gideon was confused. If God was really all-powerful, why did the Midianites seem to exercise so much power? Gideon was full of questions that had no obvious answers.

When God appeared to him, Gideon was threshing wheat in a sunken winepress, a hole designed to catch the juice of the grapes being tread. Usually this was a lower place and the threshing floor was the higher place. The men and animals would trample the wheat and then push the wheat into the air with pitchforks, and the chaff would blow away while the wheat fell.

Gideon was used to threshing wheat in open view. But now he was hiding from the Midianites, his conquerors. He was a little ashamed of himself. He didn't feel manly. He was watching the enemy take the mountaintop while he hid in the valley.

"All right, Lord," he said, "if you are with us, then why are they up there and we down here? How can I know for sure? How, in my confusion, can I know that you are with me if it seems that they are doing all right and we are having a hard time of it? We are having to lie, it seems. We are having to beguile. We are having to steal from ourselves in order to feed our children. Lord, why is this happening to us?"

Doesn't he have the right to ask? He is no useless skeptic, asking questions just to make trouble. He is a cautious man, bewildered by unfolding events. I believe this message could be relevant to us. Perhaps you have thought the same things, and the emotions have run just as deep. Here is a man who has searched the ways of God, hidden in the caves, fought for the truth, and who comes but to do the will of God. He has the right to ask. Jesus had the right to ask of his Father, "Father, why?" We have the right, too.

Some whys are going to go unanswered. Gideon wondered, "Aren't there other men in Israel God could be using? Why isn't he using the professional soldier? Why would he take a farmer?" Haven't you asked that question? Why doesn't the staff do it? Why don't some of our best teachers do that? There are so many others who could do it better than I.

Gideon went through this questioning exercise, and it was not futile on his part. It was not an excuse. It was genuine with him. He was searching his heart. When a man sees an angel face to face, he doesn't trifle with things that are sacred.

He Calls the Contrite

God calls men who are contrite.

He says in verse 15, "Oh my Lord, wherewith shall I save Israel?" What can I do? What do I have? What preparation? What weapons? What armies? What following? What training? What experience? How do I know the people will follow me? I thing the people always follow a God-anointed man. Gideon didn't know this, but he found it out.

Then, in humility, he began to say, Lord, you understand where I came from. You understand who I am. You understand my family. They are poor. They have never distinguished themselves. They have had no honors.

They have never been singled out. They have lived, they have died, they have been buried with their fathers. Nobody knows where they are buried. Nobody remembers their names or why they lived. Lord, why do you call me? I am the least of my father's.

He went on to say, "My family is the poorest in Manasseh." Manasseh wasn't the proudest tribe of Israel by any means. Speak of Judah and you speak of courage. Speak of Levi and you speak of service. Speak of Manasseh and you do not speak of family pride, tribal pride, or personal pride. Gideon had no pride, no possessions, no pretentiousness. Perhaps that is why God could use him.

God was dealing with a fearful farmer. He was not a soldier with a sword, but a man of true grit. This man of God sincerely, genuinely, contritely said, "You know that I am the least of my family, Lord. What do you want with me?" And the Lord kept on talking. He wanted a courageous man. He wanted a contrite man. He used even a confused man. He wanted a common man for an uncommon task.

"Amazing grace! how sweet the sound, That saved a wretch like me!" It is an amazing thing that God would choose us.

We need to think twice about turning down any opportunity of service. "Show me a sign, Lord," said Gideon. And he was never the same after that. May God give each of us a sign that we cannot, will not, fail to respond to—and the grit and grace adequate to the occasion.

9

JABEZ

The Prerogatives of Prayer

1 CHRONICLES 4:9–10

In a recent *Peanuts* cartoon, Linus was begging Lucy to tell him a story. Exasperated with the repeated requests, she says, "A man was born. He lived. He died." Then she walked away. Linus sits there for a moment and then ponders aloud, "Kinda makes you wonder, doesn't it?"

Lucy's answer sounds like so many of the genealogies in the Bible. "A begat B, B begat C, C begat D," and so on. Each one lived and then died. We feel so tempted to skip over them as we read. But if we do, we may miss a gem amid the dust, a real man within the halls of a wax museum.

In the middle of this passage in 1 Chronicles, there is just such a gem. In the middle of a list of men who were born, lived, and died, we read these verses:

"Jabez was more honourable than his brethren: and his mother called his name Jabez, saying, Because I bare him with sorrow.

"And Jabez called on the God of Israel, saying, 'Oh that thou wouldest bless me indeed, and enlarge my coast,

85

and that thine hand might be with me, and that thou wouldest keep me from evil, that it may not grieve me!' '' (4:9).

And the conclusion is: "God granted him that which he requested" (v. 10).

In this thumbnail sketch, we have the only picture of Jabez given in the whole Bible. But from these two verses we can see that he was a remarkable man.

Jabez had a godly ancestry. He descended from the Rechabites, whose chief, Jonadab, commanded his people to dwell in tents and abstain from intoxicants in order to preserve their virtue. Centuries later Jeremiah found this tribe still faithful to their ancestors' vow.

But the character of Jabez consisted of more than just his ancestry, of more than a vow of abstinence. His character exceeded the expectations of his mother, who "bore him with sorrow."

It is possible that Jabez received the name of "sorrowful" because he was unwanted or faced unusual hardship or poverty. Some speculate that perhaps his brothers had stolen his inheritance. His greatest handicap is indicated in the fact that his mother was the one who named him, probably a sign that his father was dead. According to custom, the father normally named the child. Yet his character developed in spite of, perhaps because of, poor beginnings.

You never can tell by a man's starting point where he will end. Some begin in glory but end in gloom. Others, like Abraham Lincoln or Andrew Jackson, begin in the shadows but end in the spotlight.

In spite of his handicap, Jabez was strong. The secret

of his strength was prayer. In prayer he turned to the father of the fatherless, the help of the helpless.

Jabez prayed intelligently. He knew that the God of Israel had made a covenant with his people. He knew that God would keep that covenant, and that he might call on him in prayer. James says we ask and receive not because we ask amiss. We must pray intelligently.

Jabez prayed earnestly. He cried out to the Lord, "Oh that thou wouldest bless me indeed!" What passion, what agony in Jabez' prayer! What an indictment of our formal, passionless, half-hearted prayers! How often have you cried aloud, "Oh, that you would bless me!" Is it any wonder our prayers are ineffectual?

Jabez prayed definitely. He knew what he wanted, and he asked for those things. If we are not specific in our requests, how will God answer so that we can know he has answered?

Jabez prayed effectively. We are told, "God granted him that which he requested." The same God who answered Jabez' prayer has pledged himself to answer ours. "Whatsoever ye shall ask the Father in my name, he will give it to you . . . ask, and ye shall receive" (John 16:23–24).

When we pray for the same things Jabez prayed for, we have the right to expect the same affirmative answer. We should use Jabez' prayer as a guide and an encouragement for our own. He made four requests that we also may make.

Grace

Jabez prayed, "Oh that thou wouldest bless me indeed." Literally this could be rendered, "Oh, that in really blessing you would really bless me." Is there a stronger way to ask for a blessing?

Jabez needed special grace to overcome the difficulties he faced. He asked for blessing because his way was bleak. His mother had so prophesied. He knew that if he were ever to be the man God wanted him to be, he would need grace, a divine enabling.

Paul came to the same conclusion. He said, "For I am the least of the apostles . . . because I persecuted the church of God. But by the grace of God I am what I am: and his grace which was bestowed upon me was not in vain; but I laboured more abundantly than they all: yet not I, but the grace of God which was with me" (1 Cor. 15:9–10). Paul did not say, "By my education, by my strength, by my heritage." He said, "By grace I am what I am."

God's grace, unmerited yet freely given, is always available to us to help us overcome our handicaps. God assured Paul, "My grace is sufficient for thee: for my strength is made perfect in weakness" (2 Cor. 12:9). These assurances are a blessing to us.

Material prosperity may mean spiritual poverty.

Material victory may mean spiritual defeat.

Material blessing is often a spiritual curse.

Spiritual blessings are true blessings. We are already wonderfully blessed, for God "hath blessed with all spiritual blessings."

In a testimonial meeting several were telling how God had transformed their lives from lawlessness, immorality, and drunkenness. At the climax of the meeting a little lady got to her feet and gave the most startling testimony of all. She said, "Jesus saved me from a life of ease, luxury, and selfishness, and it took just as much grace to save me from my easy chair as it did to save these others from the gutter."

When we ask God for true blessing, we may not get what we expect. True blessings sometimes come in the form of adversities and pain, hardship and sorrow. But in the end they may prove to be blessings indeed.

Theodore Roosevelt grew up a weak and sickly child in the midst of ease and luxury. It was only through toil and strenuous activity that he transformed himself into a whole man and a maker of destiny.

If we want real blessing, we should ask God to send it in whatever form he chooses. To do so is to pray as Jesus taught us, "Thy kingdom come, thy will be done on earth as it is in heaven."

Growth

Jabez prayed for growth. "Enlarge my coast!" he said. What a colorful image! What a wonderful expression of desire for extended boundaries, greater visions! He wanted room. He wanted his territory enlarged.

The last exhortation we have from Peter is that we "grow in grace and in the knowledge of our Lord and Saviour Jesus Christ" (2 Pet. 3:18). Too many of us are content to remain babies when we should "desire the sincere milk of the word, that [we] may grow thereby" (1 Pet. 2:2). Paul condemned the Corinthians for continuing to baby new Christians.

If a man is going to grow, going to be led of the Lord,

he must have a goal. Jabez had a dream. He had a vision
of walls pushed back, of a larger life. Our lives are only
as large as our visions. No man ever grows beyond his
goal. No man ever jumps further than he intends. His feet
may not reach the spot on which he has set his eyes, but
one thing is sure: they will never go beyond it. As
Proverbs 29:18 says, "Where there is no vision, the
people perish."

We need to pray that God will deepen our faith,
broaden our love, and heighten our hope.

We need to pray that God will give us increased oppor-
tunities for service.

We need to pray that we will grow in greater likeness
to the image of his Son (see Rom. 8:29).

W. H. Griffith-Thomas says, "The Christian life is
like riding a bicycle. If you do not go on, you go off." If
we do not grow, we decay.

Guidance

It may be that we ask only for deliverance. Let us ask
instead for guidance. Jabez prayed that the hand of God
might be with him.

On a downtown sidewalk a little girl ran ahead of her
mother until she came to a busy intersection. Then she
waited, and reached for her mother's hand. It was too
dangerous to go on alone.

Jabez reached for God's hand. There is power in the
hand of God. The Lord brought Israel out of Egypt
"through a mighty hand" (Deut. 5:15). The hand of God
is stronger than any other possible power or combination
of forces (John 10:29).

There is also punishment in the hand of God. David, in acknowledging God's chastising him for his sin, said, "Day and night thy hand was heavy upon me" (Ps. 32:4). The writer of the book of Hebrews said, "It is a fearful thing to fall into the hands of the living God" (10:31).

There is providence in the hand of God. This is what Jabez prayed for—the guidance and care that comes from having God's hand on one's shoulder.

We, too, need guidance. Life is too beset by perils for us to go alone. God has a way for us, a plan for our lives: "The steps of a man are ordered by the Lord" (Ps. 37:23). He has promised to direct us if we ask: "In all thy ways acknowledge him, and he shall direct thy paths" (Prov. 3:6).

God sent Jesus to be our guide: "I am the way," he confirmed.

Godliness

Jabez' final request was profound: "Keep me from evil, that it may not grieve me!" How well he knew the nature of sin. Of course, he could have been praying for protection from his enemies; but the greatest enemy of man is sin. It is the spoiler of life. Even the tiniest sin can throw a life out of balance.

A man was called to repair a great clock that was sometimes slow and sometimes fast. Examining it, he found nothing wrong, but thoroughly overhauled and serviced it anyway. Soon he was called again. Again he could find nothing wrong. As he was leaving, he stopped across the street to look at the clock. While he was watching, a pigeon flew up and lighted on the minute hand. He slowed the movement of the hand just enough to throw the timing off. Then he flew away, only to return as the minute hand started its ascent up the other side.

Sin is like that pigeon. Almost unnoticeably, it corrupts our lives so that something is always wrong.

Jesus taught us to pray, "Lead us not into temptation, but deliver us from evil." God wants to deliver us from evil, but he does not do it by isolating us from the world. Jesus prayed, "I pray not that thou wouldest take them out of the world, but that thou wouldest keep them from evil." It's all right for the boat to be in the water, but there's trouble when the water is in the boat. We must be in the world, but the world need not be in us.

The only way to keep evil out of our lives is to make sure that the Lord fills us completely. Man has no godliness on his own; "all our righteousness is as filthy rags." Godliness comes only from a true relationship with God. It is our only protection against godlessness.

Through faith we can say with Paul, "The Lord shall deliver me from every evil work" (2 Tim. 4:18).

Jesus tells us, "Ask, and it shall be given you." Jabez' story is proof of that. His every request was granted.

So shall ours be if we make grace, growth, guidance, and godliness our prerogatives in prayer.

10

DANIEL

The Price of Prayer

DANIEL 6:1–11

Have you asked yourself the question, Is there such a thing as a price to prayer? Does it pay, or does it cost? Perhaps we will find an answer in the story of Daniel.

Daniel's story is helpful in many ways. It has helped many a timid boy who goes away to college to put his Bible by his pillow. It has helped many a serviceman bow unashamedly at his bunk to pray before he goes to bed. It has showed many that a man can be Christian both in business and politics.

Daniel had enemies in this strange land. He did not look for them, but they found him because of his public success and his private discipline.

Daniel was not in Babylon by choice; he was there as a captive. He was brought there and kept against his will, a slave. You would think that he would have given up praying and relinquished any thought of going back to Jerusalem in the last years of his life. But Daniel was praying as he had always prayed.

If you stand for anything in life you will have some enemies, and so you ought to choose them with as much care as you would your friends. Your enemies are as much a recommendation of you as your friends in life are. Daniel had the kind of friends that will always be known as prayer-meeting friends, and that is the kind to have.

Daniel's enemies plotted against his life. As all enemies must, these had to use deception in their trap. His enemies had recognized that prayer was a habit, a way of life, and devotion the very discipline of his nature. His faith would stand up even in captivity. This, then, was where they were going to try him. His faith was well-founded and his habits were known and not new to them. Therefore they considered them. They fed the king's ego, and ego is a costly thing to feed. They knew they could not trap him in anything except his devotion toward God. They must have felt that surely this man would have given up a long while ago.

The Person of Prayer

It is believed that Daniel was eighty-five to ninety years old. He occupied the second place in the kingdom, or what we call the role of prime minister. Though Daniel had served the Babylonians as a slave, many of them respected him more than they did some of those who were serving as free men. His faith had sustained him in other days. Would it now in this new danger?

Strangely, God has often used bonds to bless. That fact is a paradox in itself. For example, I wonder how many hymns Fanny Crosby would have written if it had not been for her blindness and her dependence on God? I wonder how many epistles Paul might have written if he had not had to deal with the thorn in his flesh? He served God in spite of the thorn.

The lions are always waiting for the Christian. But such tests are the only challenge the true believer will accept. There is more peace in the lions' den than there is in the palace, because the Christian's heart is stilled by the assurance of the presence of God.

Christians are still being asked the same question the king asked Daniel the next morning. He had heard the roar of the lions in the night. Now all was quiet in the early morning dawn, and he wondered if the beasts had devoured his prophet. Anxiously he rushed to the pit and called out into the silence, "O Daniel, servant of the living God, has your God, whom you serve continually, been able to deliver you from the lions?" (Dan. 6:20, RSV).

The world is still asking that question. Does it pay to pray, or is the cost greater than the dividends? And we answer with the songwriter, "He is able." If we do God's will and leave things in his hands, surely the same God who was able to close the mouths of hungry lions will be able to handle our little problems!

The Place of Prayer

Let's think about not only the person of prayer but also the place of prayer.

You will recall that there were no temples of worship in Babylon, no houses of prayer dedicated for that purpose. It was a pagan land. Since there was no place of prayer, Daniel made himself a place—a private place. It was an open window facing Jerusalem. If you have been in the Middle East the year round, you know that he had a reason for praying by an upstairs open window. It is one of the few private places, the only place one can find a refuge from the heat. It was not unusual for there to be a period in the middle of the day to rest. Daniel used his rest time for prayer and meditation.

The window looked toward home, but it also looked toward heaven. And you can be sure that if there was an open window toward heaven in pagan Babylon, there was also an open window in heaven toward pagan Babylon.

There is a daily devotional book that has been in publication for many years now. Over the years this little book has blessed the lives of scores of people. It is a book called *Open Windows*.

It is amazing how an insignificant thing like an open window has such significance in God's Word. Smooth stones, an alabaster box, five sparrows, two mites, a rooster crowing—God uses ordinary things in extraordinary ways to change the lives of people.

All Daniel's enemies were watching his window that day. Do you think he wondered whether he should close the window? He probably did wonder. But he didn't close the window. You can be sure the God of Daniel remembered he prayed three times daily and was there to hear his prayer. If the window had been closed, would God have answered it? Not that God would have any problem hearing through a closed window, but I think Daniel would have had some difficulty praying through a closed window.

Daniel knelt humbly before God. Not that his posture

was important, but there are some problems that bring men to their knees.

A man was climbing the Alps with a guide. As the two came to a difficult part of the climb, the guide called down that from this point on they would go on their knees. Sometimes it seems we make the most progress on our knees.

That window was a witness to the faith of a man of God, a testimony to his prayer life. We can mark forever Daniel's open window because it symbolizes God's watching over his people. Daniel's prayer wasn't offered in the Temple at an appointed time; it was offered in an ordinary house and in an ordinary place. And God heard him.

The Principle of Prayer

Let us consider the principle of prayer.

I think the secret of Daniel's prayer is in the tenth verse, where it says he went to his window to pray "as he did aforetime," which means "as he usually did." The decree had been signed. Daniel was to die if he paid homage to anyone but the king. His enemies were watching. He would be turned in. Nevertheless, he prayed "as he did aforetime."

Daniel taught us how to pray in a time of calm as well as a time of crisis. God was Daniel's only friend in captivity; he turned to him unashamedly. Would God not listen to one who had been praying three times a day before the crisis? He had been doing the righteous thing so long he did not think of changing his ways. Prayer was a principle with Daniel. And, knowing that here was a man who could be depended upon, God left open the windows of heaven.

When the *Titanic,* that luxury passenger vessel sailing under the British flag, was sinking, the captain sent for his officers. The last thing he said to them on the bridge was, "Men, be men; be British." There should be a few principles we would be willing to die for, and times of crisis can be met with brave hearts if we are people of prayer. Perhaps Daniel's words to us would be, "Be men and women of courage; be Christian."

How does the story end?

Daniel 9:22 says, "He came and said he to me, O Daniel, I have now come out to give you wisdom and understanding. At the beginning of your supplications a word went forth, and I have come to tell it to you, for you are greatly beloved" (RSV). God greatly loves a man who keeps the doors and windows of his heart and house open to heaven.

11

A PHARISEE

The Presumptuous Prayer

LUKE 18:9–14

In old-time melodrama, one could always recognize the villain by his black attire and mustache. The hero was handsome and wore white, and was applauded as soon as he came onstage, while the villain was hissed and booed.

The parable of the Pharisee and the publican may have been intended to be a melodrama, so exaggerated do the roles of each seem to be. But we no longer see the characters as Jesus' listeners did. To them the Pharisee was the hero, the "good guy in the white hat," the bastion of Judaism. The publican was the villain—traitor, coward, crook. The publican might have been the Gentile of the day.

If we sigh to ourselves and say, "Lord, I thank thee that I am not as that Pharisee," we will have missed the point completely. We will be as guilty of blindness as the Pharisee. Rather, we should put ourselves in his place.

Actually, the Pharisees were the most admired men of their day. In religious circles everyone looked up to them. They were champions of the faith. The Sadducees were the liberals, the skeptics; they didn't believe in resurrection.

Look at this Pharisee in the Temple. We might admire him, too. We could admire his orthodoxy, for he believed the letter of the law.

This Pharisee was well-disciplined. In an era of luxury and loose living, he held high the standard of virtue. He denounced worldliness and compromise.

He was generous. He tithed, which is more than many Christians today do. He tithed of his produce and his income as well. From the Pharisee we learn the principle of giving to the maximum instead of doing the minimum. Doesn't the Lord want us to do our most, not our least?

Finally, he was a sort of supersaint, noted for his fasting and prayers, and dedicated and devoted to God's work. Certainly we can admire his devotion.

Yet, for all we can say positively for this Pharisee, we must agree with Clovis Chappell that he was a "decent devil." Everything about him was decent. He dressed neatly. His standing in the community was excellent. He was respectable in every way. He only gave himself away when he began to pray.

Perhaps that is true of most of us. What was it about his prayer that revealed his attitude?

A Disdainful Prayer

First, his prayer was disdainful. He made the same mistake as the little girl who prayed, "Our Father who art in heaven, how does He know my name!" Unconsciously, his prayer was self-centered. He moved as close to the altar as he could so that he would be sure to be seen. Most men did not dare to stand too close to the holy

place, but he wanted the attention. His attitude was one
of conceit.

Verse 9 says he also "despised others." He counted
others as nothing. Their opinions he valued little; their
lives were worthless. He felt that God could not possibly
love them as God loved him. His pride caused him to
elevate himself above others by belittling them. But how
can a man be spiritual and debase others at the same
time?

I am reminded of the prayer of Rabbi Simeon Ben
Jochai, who prayed, "Lord, if there are only two righteous men in the world, I and my son are these two; if
there is only one, I am he!" The Pharisee lifted himself
up by putting others down: "Lord, I thank thee that I am
not as other men." Quite a difference from the prayer of
the publican, who in essence muttered, "God, I thank
thee that other men are not as I am."

The Pharisee as a class is extinct, but the spirit is alive
and thriving. There are so many of us today whose
thoughts are only of ourselves. Our prayers are filled with
I, I, I. Anyone who is so full of himself has little room
for others, much less for God.

A Deceptive Prayer

The Pharisee's prayer was also self-deceptive. First
John 1:8 says, "If we say we have no sin, we deceive
ourselves." Yet the Pharisee didn't feel guilty of any sin.
There was no sense of the need to confess.

A layman once told me that he hated to hear a certain
man pray in public because he never asked God to forgive him of any sin, nor did he lead the congregation to

seek forgiveness. He never felt the need because he never felt he had done anything morally wrong. Surely this man was deceiving himself, for we "all have sinned and come short of the glory of God." No prayer is acceptable unless we seek forgiveness.

There was no confession in the Pharisee's prayer. On the contrary, he praised his own merits. Instead of being "weighed in the balance and found wanting," he saw himself as measuring up and with merit to spare.

When he compared himself with others, he chose the worst of men at that—thieves, adulterers, and especially the publican. Not only did he see no vices in himself; he numbered his virtues as being over and above the required.

Aren't we all guilty of this? Don't we all make ourselves look good by comparing ourselves to others? Yet we are careful whom we choose for the comparison!

It is easy to find someone who compares unfavorably, who seems worse than we are. But other men are not to be our standard. We are to measure ourselves against perfection. Surely, all of us can point to some good we have done, but if we compare ourselves to the ultimate good, to the life of Jesus Christ, how do we stack up? "Be ye therefore perfect, even as your Father which is in heaven is perfect," says Matthew 5:48.

William Barclay tells of taking the train from Scotland down to England. As the train passed through the Yorkshire moors, Barclay saw a little cottage whose whiteness seemed dazzling against the grayish-purple of the rolling moors. On the return to Scotland, snow had fallen and blanketed the countryside. Now the little cottage seemed drab and soiled, almost gray in comparison with the pristine whiteness of the snow.

Compared to other men, we may appear as white as that little cottage. But measured against the purity and goodness of the Father, we fall far short; our whiteness is soiled.

There was no confession in the Pharisee's prayer, and there was no thanksgiving. He did say, "I thank thee," but there was no real gratitude; for God had really not given him what he was thanking for. What he really meant was, "God, you ought to be thankful that I am not as other men are."

How often we fail to thank God for what he has already given us, for prayers already answered. How often we approach the throne of grace with arrogance, as if to say, "Look how lucky you are, God, that I am here today!"

Third, there is no petition in the Pharisee's prayer. He feels no need. He asks for nothing because he is not aware that he needs any help. God has nothing to give him; he is self-sufficient. And he certainly would not petition on anyone else's behalf; he is too wrapped up in his own worth.

Do we come on Sundays out of habit, and not because we feel the need? Do we come because we want to impress others with our holiness? Do we come without any burden of sin, or any desire to pray for our fellows who might be suffering or lost?

A man dreamed that he went into a church just as the janitor was closing up. It was nearly dark in the building. Near the roof the man saw some birds fluttering about, trying to get out of the church. The man asked the janitor, "What are they?" and the janitor replied, "They are some of the prayers which were offered here today. They will never reach God for they were mere words."

The Bible tells us "the Pharisee prayed with himself." Surely this is true, for he was not really praying at all. He was merely talking to himself. Is this the way we pray?

A Dangerous Prayer (v. 14)

Because the Pharisee's prayer was deceptive, it was also dangerous. It ignored his need. He was blind to the fact that there was anything wrong.

In any area of life the first step toward improvement is a recognition of need. Unless we admit our inability, we cannot be helped. As someone said, "God cannot save peacocks." One cannot strut to Calvary; he must come on his hands and knees.

The Pharisee used religion as a cosmetic. He was adept at hiding his blemishes; he refused to ask for the healing of God. But there is a vast difference in being whitewashed and in being washed white. Perhaps the only thing worse in the sight of God than being a sinner is not admitting that you are one.

Another danger in the Pharisee's prayer was that he placed his trust in the wrong place. He trusted in himself, in his own good works, for righteousness. Isn't that what self-righteousness implies—that we can be righteous in and of ourselves? But that is like hiding under your own shadow; it can't be done! How can imperfect human beings rely on themselves for perfection?

A person displeased with a photograph of herself complained to the photographer that the picture didn't do her justice. The photographer replied, "It isn't justice you need, but mercy." The Pharisee wanted to plead his case before God's bar of justice. "Look, I have done this and this and this. Thank God, I am better than the rest." What the Pharisee needed, and failed to recognize that he needed, was mercy.

Everything we have in our possession we got in one of three ways. We either were given it, earned it, or stole it. But righteousness is a possession we can neither steal nor earn. It is only a gift of God. And we can only have that gift by ceasing to trust in ourselves and trusting in God instead. Jesus alone can give us the righteousness that God will accept.

The final danger of the Pharisee's prayer was that it showed his oblivion to the urgency of the situation. He returned from the house of God just as he was. Nothing about him had changed.

A lost man once said to me, "I have no fear. I will be in the hands of a merciful God." How can we expect mercy when we have nothing but scorn for God and for men? The Pharisee needed to be "justified through grace"—changed—by God. He needed to be accepted "just as he was."

Jesus Christ justifies us before God; he presents us to God just as we are and intercedes on our behalf. But only if we first recognize our need and then place our trust in him.

12

STEPHEN

The Princely Prayer

ACTS 7:55–60

One of the classics of literature is Charles Dickens' *A Tale of Two Cities*. In a moving scene at the end of the book, Sydney Carton, a reprobate all his life, performs the first noble act of his career. Taking the place of his rival in jail, he gives up his life so the woman he loves can have the man she loves. Those who witness his death at the guillotine later report, "It was the peacefullest man's face ever beheld there." The sublime look on his face revealed the calm of his heart.

Acts 7 tells of a man who faced death in the same way. In the midst of stoning by a violent mob, his was the "face of an angel." That man was Stephen.

What kind of man was Stephen?

Selected as one of the later disciples, he was a man of "honest report, full of the Holy Ghost and wisdom."

He was a man full of "power [who], did great wonders and miracles among the people." He was also a man "full of faith" (see Acts 6).

Full of faith, power, wisdom, and the Holy Spirit, Stephen was one of the first deacons and an outstanding

preacher. But perhaps he is best remembered as the first
Christian martyr because his death, like that of Jesus
Christ, was not a defeat but a victory! One of the most
celebrated subjects of Christian art through the centuries,
Stephen fulfilled the promise of his name, *Stephanos,*
which means "crown." Jesus had promised, "Be thou
faithful unto death, and I will give thee a crown of life."

Triumph Over Fear (vv. 55–56)

The story of Stephen's death is recorded in Acts
7:55–60. An effective preacher, he had angered the
people with his words. They were "cut to the heart" with
his accusations that they were responsible for the death of
Jesus. And so they sought to do away with him, to quiet
him lest he disturb their consciences.

Unable "to resist the wisdom and the spirit by which
he spake," they blasphemed against him, stirred up the
elders and scribes of the church, and brought him before
the council to be tried. When the high priest asked him to
account for himself, he began with the history of the
Jewish people.

He recounted the deeds of Moses and the faithlessness
of the people, reminding his accusers of the idol worship
of their ancestors. When he had laid the groundwork, he
turned to tell them: "Ye stiffnecked and uncircumcised in
heart and ears, ye do always resist the Holy Ghost: as
your fathers did, so do ye" (7:51).

Infuriated by the accusations and the truth of his
words, the council snarled at him like wild animals. They
covered their ears with their hands, unable to hear the
truth. Stung into action, they "ran upon him with one

accord.'' But Stephen, ''being full of the Holy Ghost, looked up stedfastly into heaven, and saw the glory of God, and Jesus standing on the right hand of God.'' Stephen's *outlook* may have been bad, but his *uplook* was glorious.

Sometimes it takes a dark outlook to make us interested in looking up. Remember Isaiah? It was ''in the year that King Uzziah died''—a year of turmoil for his people—that Isaiah saw the Lord ''high and lifted up'' (Isa. 6).

Remember Eddie Rickenbacker? When he was adrift on the ocean and death seemed near, he saw the Lord.

Exalting Christ is a crime which the world will not leave unpunished. Timothy reminds us, ''All that will live godly in Christ Jesus shall suffer persecution.'' Each time we stand up for Jesus we will face the same opposition Stephen faced—not as extreme, perhaps, but just as real, and an ostracism just as difficult to accept. Witness and martyr are the same word in Greek. One will pay the price for being a follower of Jesus.

Stephen stood courageously as they attacked him. Perhaps he had heard the words of Jesus, ''Fear not them which kill the body, but are not able to kill the soul'' (Matt. 10:28). Perhaps he was foretelling the words of Paul, ''To live is Christ, to die is gain.''

Perhaps he remembered the verses from the Sermon on the Mount: ''Blessed are ye, when men shall revile you, and persecute you, and shall say all manner of evil against you falsely, for my sake . . . great is your reward in heaven'' (Matt. 5:11–12).

A man in Colombia was taken by twenty others and

buried up to his head in a grave. They demanded he change his political party and his religion. He agreed to change his political party because he considered that of no consequence, but he refused to change religions. They threatened loudly. "If I can win more souls by dying than by living," he cried out, "then I am ready to die, Lord!" Enraged, one of the tormentors shot him in the head. Three weeks later, fifteen of the twenty persecutors accepted Christ as Savior and joined an evangelical church.

The Christian who faces opposition and death courageously wins a great victory over fear!

Triumph of Faith (v. 59)

Charles Haddon Spurgeon tells of the unbeliever who boasted to a Christian, "Some of you Christians have great fear in dying because you believe that there is another state to follow this one. I have not the slightest fear, for I believe that I shall be annihilated."

"Yes," replied the Christian, "and in that respect you seem to me to be on equal terms with that bull grazing over there which, like yourself is free from any fear of death. Pray, sir, let me ask you a simple question. Have you any hope?"

"Hope, sir? Hope? Of course, I have no hope."

"Ah, then," replied the Christian, "despite the fears that sometimes come over feeble believers, they have a hope which they could not and would not give up."

It matters less that a man face death courageously than that he face it hopefully.

We all face death. If we are realistic, we face it now. Do you have any hope? If Christ lives in you, the answer is yes. If he does not, the answer is no. "Christ in you," wrote Paul, "the hope of glory" (Col. 1:27).

The time to get ready for death is before it faces you. Augustine noted one case of deathbed repentance in the Bible—the thief on the cross. That case is there so that we will not despair; but it is the only one there—so that we will not presume.

Matthew Henry further says, "True repentance is never too late, but late repentance is seldom true."

Are we ready for death?

The crowd dragged Stephen from the city and stoned him. In faith he cried aloud, "Lord Jesus, receive my spirit." His was the faith of the Son of God, who from the cross said, "Into thy hands I commend my spirit." For Stephen, as for Jesus, death was filled with certainties: the certainty of immortality, the certainty that God is near, the certainty that there is safety in his hands, and that he is both willing and able to receive.

Notice that Stephen cried out to *Jesus*. Alexander Maclaren writes, "Strange that a dying man should cry thus to a dead man who had been unable to save himself." Would Stephen have cried aloud to Jesus had he not been convinced of his Lord's resurrection?

These same certainties that Stephen had are ours if we claim them.

Notice the other similarities between the deaths of Jesus and Stephen.

Both were falsely accused.

Both appeared before the same council.

Both prayed for forgiveness for their executioners. "Lay not this sin to their charge," cried Stephen. How reminiscent of Jesus' words of love, "Father, forgive them, for they know not what they do."

What does this mean? It means that Stephen was so devoted to Jesus that he modeled him in death.

Stephen's death is the only detailed account we have of martyrdom in the New Testament. James the apostle is dismissed in a single statement; nothing is said of Peter or Paul. What does this tell us? The implication is that how a man lives is more important than how he died. If we live life well, death will take care of itself, and through faith, death can be a victory. Stephen's certainties can be ours. Stephen's faith can be ours. May we model our Lord in life even as Stephen did in death.

Triumph of Forgiveness (v. 60)

Stephen's last cry was for forgiveness, but not for himself. He had already made his peace with God long before. Stephen prayed for forgiveness for those who were killing him.

What a difference the coming of Christ makes! The last Old Testament martyr was Zechariah, who told the people the Lord had forsaken them because they had forsaken the Lord. Enraged, the king ordered his death, and as Zechariah lay dying, he cried in a loud voice, "May the Lord see and avenge!" (2 Chron. 24:22, RSV).

"Revenge is sweet" is a common saying; but in truth, nothing sours faster. The ravages of reconstruction in the south are a bitter example of the fruit of revenge.

Forgiveness brings forth sweet fruit. Stephen prayed, "Lord, lay not this sin to their charge." The blood of the martyrs watered the seeds of the faith that produced Christians for generations to follow. Do you remember that when Christ prayed for forgiveness for his tormentors, the centurion was saved? When Stephen prayed, a young man named Saul stood near, and the wheels were set in motion that led to his conversion. Says Augustine of that moment in history, "The church owes Paul to the prayer of Stephen."

"What did God do for Stephen?" a scoffer asked Joseph Parker. "He gave him the power to pray for those who stoned him," Dr. Parker replied.

Only Jesus can give us the power to truly forgive; only Jesus can give us the power to triumph over fear and death.

We should live and introduce Christ to people in such a way that he is unforgettable. If we show the courage, the faith, and the forgiveness of Stephen, we will triumph in the end.

13

PAUL

The Perplexity of Prayer

2 CORINTHIANS 12:7–10

"Victory through prayer" is the motto of our church. It is inscribed on the cornerstone of the auditorium. It is carved on the beam in the prayer chapel. It is printed on the church materials we use.

What does "victory through prayer" mean?

When we think of victorious prayer, we probably recall some dramatic example such as the experience of Captain Eddie Rickenbacker, who was lost at sea with seven other men. In answer to their prayers for food, God sent a sea gull who landed on the top of Rickenbacker's head; in answer to their requests for water, God sent rain. And after twenty-one days, God answered their prayer for rescue.

But is all prayer so victorious?

Sometimes we pray earnestly and nothing happens. It seems as though our prayers have been for nought. Even in the case of Rickenbacker and his crew, one man was lost. Even their prayers were not answered as they might have wished.

Parents pray for a sick child, and the child grows

119

worse and dies.

A wife prays for her lost husband, but he remains unconverted.

The church prays for the spiritual safety of its young people and they go astray and fall into sin.

Each of us could cite examples of our own in which we feel that our own prayers have gone unanswered. If we were to make two lists, one of answered and one of unanswered prayers, I wonder which would be the longer.

Prayer is perplexing. Which of us understands why some prayers are answered and others seemingly are not? The perplexity is compounded by the fact that God has promised to answer prayer. In Jeremiah 33:3 he says, "Call unto me and I will answer thee." In Matthew Jesus tells his listeners, "Ask and it shall be given you" (7:7). And in John 14:13 we read, "Whatsoever ye shall ask in my name, that will I do."

We have the impression from reading the Psalms that David constantly enjoyed answered prayer. "Thou hast given him his heart's desire, thou hast not withholden the request of his lips" (21:2).

Yet our own experience seems more like that of the young boy in Somerset Maugham's *Of Human Bondage*. The child was greatly distressed about being handicapped with a club foot. His parents assured him that, if he prayed earnestly, his prayer would be answered immediately. That night the boy did pray, earnestly and in faith, that his foot would be cured while he slept. He believed so strongly that the miracle would occur that when he awoke the next morning, he lay there basking in the joy of being healed. It was a traumatic discovery to push back the covers and see that his foot was just as it had been the night before.

What are we saying, then? That what the Bible teaches is contrary to our own experience? That it is unrealistic? That God no longer answers prayers? Even Martin Luther once cried out, "My God, art thou dead?"

What is the answer to the perplexing question of unanswered prayer?

Misconception

The answer to the problem is not in the heavens but in our heads. When it comes to prayer, we have many misconceptions.

First, the Bible does not teach that every request is fulfilled. The Bible is as full of unanswered prayers as it is of answered ones.

Moses prayed to enter the Promised Land but died on the east of Jordan.

David, in the psalm following the one already quoted, cried out, "O my God, I cry in the daytime, but thou hearest not" (22:2).

Jeremiah called out in his lamentation, "Thou hast covered thyself with a cloud, that our prayer should not pass through" (Lam. 3:44).

The prophet Habakkuk complained, "O Lord, how long shall I cry, and thou wilt not hear?" (Hab. 1:2).

Even Jesus was denied his request that he be spared the cross.

One of the best examples of petitions turned down is God's refusal to remove Paul's "thorn in the flesh" after three requests!

Paul was no spiritual newcomer; he was a spiritual giant. He wrote much of the New Testament and started more churches than any other man. He suffered hardship, persecution, and shipwreck for the cause of Christ. Even so, God said no. And Paul went on serving and suffering to the end of his days. As Harry Emerson Fosdick says, he was "compelled to make the best of it and to let it make the best of him."

So, the Bible is not out of touch with reality, but our misconceptions of the Bible are. Petitions are not always granted.

Another misconception we have is of prayer itself. When we think of prayer, what do we think of first? Of petition, of asking for something. Too often that is our only concept of prayer.

How long would our families last, how deep would our relationships be if all we had in common was the requests we made of each other? Likewise, there is more to our relationship with God than our requests of him. There is much more to prayer than petition. The book of Psalms, which is the prayer book as well as the praise book of the Bible, reveals a wide range of prayers.

There are prayers of adoration: "Bless the Lord, O my soul: and all that is within me, bless his holy name" (103:1).

There are prayers of confession: "For I acknowledge my transgressions: and my sin is ever before me" (51:3).

There are prayers of thanksgiving: "At midnight I will rise to give thanks unto thee" (119:62).

There are prayers of consecration: "Teach me, O

Lord, the way of thy statutes . . . and I shall observe it with my whole heart" (119:33–34).

There are prayers of communion: "The Lord is my shepherd" (23:1).

So there is much more to prayer than mere petition. To give up praying because of unanswered requests would be like giving up driving because you came to one road-block. There is more than one avenue by which to get the full benefit of prayer.

However, making our requests known to God is an important part of prayer. We should not minimize it. In the Model Prayer Jesus made three requests: "Give us this day our daily bread. . . ." "Forgive us our tres-passes. . . ." "Deliver us from evil. . . ."

Our misconceptions are part of the answer to the perplexity of prayer, but not the whole answer.

Misuse

Another reason for the existence of unanswered prayer is our misuse of it. James says, "Ye ask, and receive not, because ye ask amiss" (Jas. 4:3).

Many of our prayers are doomed for denial from the start because they spring from our own selfish ambitions and desires for pleasure. One French king prayed to be allowed to sin "one more time."

We do not ring God up and tell him what we want like we do room service in a hotel. When we pray "my will be done" rather than "thy will be done," the only answer we get is our own echo.

Another way we misuse prayer is to ask God for something while harboring known sin in our lives. The psalmist says, "If I regard iniquity in my heart, the Lord will not hear me" (66:18).

If our prayers are not answered, we should first look for the fault in ourselves. We may not be following the conditions God has set up. If the bride ruins her first dinner for her husband, she doesn't blame her mother's recipes. She knows the fault is hers for failing to follow directions. If we do not follow God's directions, especially as regards sin, we misuse prayer and should not expect an answer.

We most frequently misuse prayer, not through selfishness but through ignorance. How many times does God have to say to us, as Jesus said to the mother of James and John, "Ye know not what ye ask" (Matt. 20:22).

Often it is a sign of God's love for us that he says no to our requests. Perhaps it would be more accurate if, instead of calling prayers unanswered, we just came to recognize no as an answer. Sometimes God has to refuse our request in order to give us what we really want.

In his *Confessions* Augustine tells how his mother Monica prayed all night that he might not sail for Italy. Augustine was not a Christian, and she was afraid that he would never become one if he left her influence and went to that place of great temptations. But God did not grant her request. While she was still praying, Augustine sailed for Italy. Yet, while he was in Italy he met Ambrose, who persuaded him to become a Christian. God denied her request as she had made it, but gave her what she really wanted.

How many of our prayers are as unwise as hers? How

gracious is God that he does not give us everything we pray for!

Perhaps the most serious misuse of prayer is to pray when we should get to work. When the Israelites were trapped between the Egyptians and the Red Sea, Moses went to pray. The Lord told Moses, "Quit praying and get the people moving" (Ex. 14:15, *The Living Bible, Paraphased*). Prayer is important, but there is a time for prayer to cease and work to begin.

An old proverb says, "If wishes were horses, beggars would ride." If all our wishes were granted immediately, God would be nothing more than a genie and we would be pampered Aladdins wishing we didn't have to rub the lamp so hard.

Our development demands our efforts. I like what Spurgeon said: "Pray to God but keep the hammer going."

Mistake

Because of our misuse of prayer, some prayers do receive negative answers. However, we often mistake an answered prayer for an unanswered one because we do not recognize the answer when it comes.

Not all of us have been given the wisdom that God gave Paul. Paul realized that, although his affliction had not been removed, God had answered his prayer by giving him something much better: his own grace and strength.

Although God does sometimes have to say no, more often he says, "No, but . . . " He may not give us what we ask, but he will give us a substitute which is much better.

God never says no to us like tired parents who mean they don't want to be bothered. To each no is linked an alternative which is greater than what we requested.

When God says no, rejoice. It means that you will receive something greater than you asked.

Henry Jowett writes, "The unremoved thorn does not mean the unanswered prayer. There was not less thorn but more grace."

We sometimes pray, as Paul did, for a change in circumstances. But God often chooses to change us rather than the circumstances. It is through circumstances that he molds us.

Gaston Foote says, "Far from getting people out of trouble, God gets people into trouble." It is when we are feeling desperate that we are made to become what we ought to be. Foote continues: "God's purpose is not to make life easy, but to make men strong; not to make us happy but to make us holy."

Paul gave up trying to overcome God's no and laid hold of God's yes. He found the answer, not in healing, but in helping.

If your car has difficulty climbing a hill, you can do one of two things: (1) make the hill less steep, or (2) increase the horsepower of the car. God usually wants to change us, not the hill.

"Who rises from prayer a better man," wrote George Meredith, "his prayer is answered."

Sometimes we mistake an answered prayer for an unanswered one because God sends a substitute.

We seek a thing and God gives us a chance.

We seek relief and God gives us strength.

We seek a "want" and God fills a need.

In a sense, then, there is no such thing as unanswered prayer.

At the close of his life Adoniram Judson said, "I never prayed sincerely and earnestly for anything, but it came; at some time—no matter how distant a day—somehow, in some shape . . . it came."

Judson prayed to enter India but was forced to go to Burma.

He prayed for his wife's life, but had to bury her and his two children.

He prayed for release from prison, but lay there months chained and miserable.

Scores of petitions went without an *affirmative* answer, but he always answered. God was with him. Perhaps that, after all, is the answer to the perplexity of prayer: that what we really need is not what we ask, but God himself.